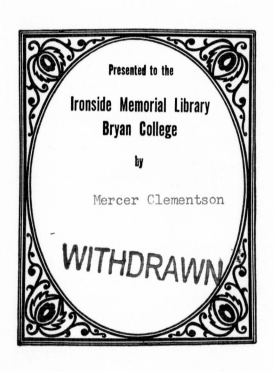

Photograph by Arnold Newman

WILLIAM S. WHITE
author of CITADEL: The Story of the U.S. Senate

Books by William S. White

THE TAFT STORY

CITADEL, The Story of the U.S. Senate

CITADEL

THE STORY OF THE U.S. SENATE

BY WILLIAM S. WHITE

HARPER & BROTHERS, PUBLISHERS, NEW YORK

Library of Congress catalog card number: 56-11089

To my daughters, Lucia and Victoria White

CONTENTS

FOREWORD

For a long time I have felt that the one touch of authentic genius in the American political system, apart, of course, from the incomparable majesty and decency and felicity of the Constitution itself, is the Senate of the United States.

I have not, at the same time, been unaware of the criticisms and the circumstances—for some of which the Senate itself is inescapably responsible—that have in our lifetime beaten so heavily upon the moral credit of the place.

It is a place upon whose vitality and honor will at length rest the whole issue of the kind of society that we are to maintain.

As I see it, the Institution very often reflects the best instincts, and very infrequently the worst instincts, of the whole long political tradition with which the Anglo-American race (and all its valued assimilated members now merged altogether in the agreeably quarrelsome unity that enriches us all) has endowed the world.

What has been this endowment? Not so much the forms and organs of government as the spirit of independent tolerance and contentious comity of a stream of political thought and practice. The indispensable characteristic of it all perhaps can be summed up by saying that the Senate is in a sense a high assembly but that in a deeper sense it is a great and unique human consensus of individual men.

At all events, this is the view I have had. Accordingly, I have approached the Institution in these terms; the attempt has been to deal with it, with all its strengths and all its weaknesses, rather as one would try to deal with the story of an extraordinary and significant man.

This being the purpose, and the writing of academic history being no part of the purpose, I have acted upon limitations about which I should like to be clear: Any Senator studied here is studied for some aspect of character and attitude that illustrates a substantially timeless aspect of the place itself. Jones in this book is Jones the Senate man; and to the tale it is not vitally important whether he is in the Senate now or left it on some yesterday or other. Thus, no great care has been or will be taken, in writing of a forum where the attrition of age and misfortune runs a fast race, to be quite exact about yesterday and today, to use with much precision such expressions as "the late" and "the former."

So far as I am concerned they are all, and will go on being, Senators of the United States.

WILLIAM S. WHITE
Washington

CITADEL

I

THE TONE

AND THE TIMELESSNESS

PRESIDENT George Washington, as the story goes, once vowed he'd be damned if he ever went to that place again. In the long years since, many others of high and low station have felt much the same way. Still, like George Washington before them, and all the country before them, they have had to deal and still have to deal with that place, which is the Senate of the United States.

It is a body like no other. For taken altogether in all its mixed attributes it has a final face that is much more human than organizational. Toward it this book looks sympathetically, but without sentimentality, as upon an old, complicated, but on the whole worthy and venerable figure. Nor is this to be a course in civics; the hope is simply to offer understanding of the complexity and simplicity and virility of something unique and fundamentally changeless in American life.

This is a celebration of an Institution that lives in an unending yesterday where the past is never gone, the present never quite decisive and the future rarely quite visible. It has its good moments and its bad moments, but to the United States it symbolizes, if nothing else at all, the integrity of continuity and wholeness.

This, the Senate of the United States, is an odd, mixed place. It is hard and efficient, and it is soft and dawdling. It is harsh, and it is kind. It is dignity, and it is disorder. It is arrogant, and it is humble. It believes in a kind of democracy (though the precise kind is a tale in itself) but it is in some things majestically undemocratic. It halts usurpations, and it usurps. It honors the system, and it rejects the system.

It is in theory a sixth of the Federal whole, one-half of the Legislative Branch, which in turn is one-third of the triune Government. But it snubs the other half of the one-third, the House of Representatives, and with great if instinctive determination it competes with another one-third, the Executive Branch headed by the White House. Only to the Supreme Court of all governmental instrumentalities does the Senate offer a real, if constrained, respect. The attitude, which is mutual, is compulsive and inevitable. Each, Senate and Court, has a historical awareness, through all the swaying clashes of political life, of the great repository and guardian of tradition that is the other.

Making the law, in conjunction with the House of Representatives, is only one of the functions of the Institution. There is the making or shaping of high policy in Senate debate. There is the vast power of investigation, the partial control even of foreign policy, and, of course, the power to judge impeachment actions against even a President. Over the affairs of the Republic, in short, the mandate of the Senate is for practical purposes limitless.

Paradox is another of the characteristics. This is a place of tidiness and it is not for tidy men. This is a place so human that it is in a sense alien altogether to government. This is a place where men may be meanly slandered but also greatly defended. This is a place where a Bilbo of Mississippi will rise with unmistakable insult to a whole race. But it is also a place where a Stennis, also of Mississippi,

3

the product of this Institution at its best, will unhesitatingly and against every hazard do his duty to his State, to his country and to his tradition, his soft voice drowning and making irrelevant the strident echoes of the voice that came before.

This is a place where many men will not let the law say plainly what the Court itself has implied in behalf of one minority. But it is also a place where these same men will risk the wrath of their most powerful backers to lift that minority from literal darkness through rural electrification; from literal cold through public housing; and from literal hunger through the farm subsidy and the subsidies that wipe out tenancy.

This is a place where the "safe" and conservative will sometimes take the lead in great and dangerous innovations, as in 1955 so patriarchal a Senator as Walter Franklin George of Georgia encouraged the Eisenhower Administration to begin negotiations with world Communism.

This is a place where men's rights are sometimes trampled upon, as in the frequent denial of the elementary right to have counsel and to confront one's accusers. But it is also a place where these rights are upheld, sometimes even against the pressures of the whole country, as when so unlikely a pair as the late Senator Taft of Ohio and former Senator Pepper of Florida, the one a conservative and the other a brightly flaming liberal, defied everybody but the men

4

themselves to prevent a military draft of striking railroad workers a decade ago.

This is a place where one member will be forgiven anything or everything and another will be forgiven hardly anything at all. There is no way of saying why this is so, except to recall the couplet about the unhappy physician: "I do not love thee, Dr. Fell. The reason why I cannot tell."

There is, moreover, no fixed definition, or example, of what is properly Senatorial. For illustration, old Senator Tom Connally of Texas was, in appearance, quintessentially what one would suppose a Senator should be. His head was leonine, heavily shocked with smooth gray-white hair. He wore a black string tie, narrowed trousers, a long black coat that just missed being a frock coat. But when he opened his mouth he fractured all the Senate's rules of elaborate courtesy just as he assaulted, out of what was in fact an excellent classical education, every rule of proper English.

In debate, in this, the world's greatest forum of debate, he was colloquial in the extreme and he had the habit of cheerfully and grandly spurning such small facts as might be inconvenient or annoying to his case. He was as unpredictable as an undischarged Roman candle, and men walked warily but still fondly about him. On an occasion in which the Republicans were attacking Democratic policy toward Nationalist China, Connally, a faithful Democrat and a statesman under his deliberately ungrammatical exterior, said, in substance, of the Nationalist Generalissimo Chiang Kai-shek:

"Ole Chiang stole three hundred million dollars in gold and fled to Formosa."

There was, of course, a great outcry at this but Connally stalked haughtily from the floor, refusing to make answer. He let it be known later that he proposed next day to acknowledge error. Reappearing then with an imitation of humble chagrin he addressed the chair to this effect:

"Mr. President, I stated on yesterday that ole Chiang had fled to Formosa with three hundred million dollars in gold. I was in error, Mr. President: Ole Chiang stole *five hundred million dollars* in gold."

Another infinitely less aggressive Senator of irreproachable manners may be constantly and mysteriously in disfavor. As has so often been said, it is one sense a club, in that men weigh and judge their fellow members, saying nevei a word but somehow emitting emanations meaning: He will do; or, He won't do.

A George of Georgia or a Millikin of Colorado may act and speak precisely as he pleases. Mr. George, for example, in his day sometimes plainly and entirely successfully told the Senate it would now proceed at once to do what he wished it to do. But others may not dare such a course.

All gather, however, in unspoken affection for the strong thrust of individualism in this sometimes stuffy body. This,

6

indeed, is one of the points where the Senate, so native as it is, is so at variance with current American life. In this great era of the manager, Senators, even very conservative ones, have no instinctive touch or taste for management. Ponderous as some may be on the floor, they are all, in the generality, actually closer to the artistic than to the business temperament.

They are, for the most part, men of many skills within whom specialization is absent, men operating important enterprises with no boards of directors, no legal counsel, and usually no public-relations men upon whom to lean. They run, each in his own way, their own show, and the best of them do it so casually and with such genial lack of visible order as to show that theirs is a talent and not a technique. Each man, in the highest moments of his career, is all but alone.

The more or less typical Senator is not really in sympathy with the folklore of "business," however he may support the concept that business must be fostered. Thus the early difficulties that some of President Eisenhower's businessmen's Cabinet had with the Senate primarily were not ideological. They were mainly human difficulties: Charles Wilson's initial breezy and unconscious patronage of Senate committees did him a good deal more harm than his controversial decisions as Secretary of Defense.

The trouble was that Wilson understandably was proud of a past success that did not much impress the Senate.

7

Vaguely and in a restricted sense it honors success of that kind but it inclines—even the irreproachably conservative part of it—to the view that Senator Duff of Pennsylvania once expressed to me with deliberate exaggeration.

"Any damn fool," said Duff, a sensitive and brilliant politician in the large frame of a collegiate right guard, "can make a million dollars."

A sense of aloneness, which is father to the corollary sense of clannish solidarity, animates the place. It is skeptical of any President, because he is, or ought to be, a manager, an administrator. It regards the House of Representatives as overmanaged, docile and not *creative*. It walks apart, very often, from the country itself. For the Senate is both indrawn and ingrown, for all that it operates upon one of the world's great lighted parliamentary stages. It has, of course, been changed in some ways through the years, particularly since its membership has become popularly elected and not appointed by the legislatures and "the big people." At bottom, however, it is adamantly unchanged: Still it looks warily at people in the mass. It fears and distrusts what some of the forefathers called "the mob."

Since the beginning of the Republic the Presidency has on the whole been essentially forward-looking though not necessarily progressive in the strictly political sense. But the Senate, if one settles upon its general tone, has been essentially backward-looking, though not necessarily reactionary in the political sense. Of course, it has known untypical moments when, for a time, it has moved out ahead of the Executive. Conversely, the Presidency has known *its* untypical moments when it has lagged behind in brief, fitful affairs of the heart with the past.

Generally speaking, however, the Presidency has been occupied with the new—look, for example, at President Jefferson's Louisiana Purchase and Andy Jackson's quarrel with the banking industry. But the Senate, with great philosophic resource, has been preoccupied with constancy to the old.

The Senate looks upon the White House as a place for the innovator, the man always tinkering about with things that might well be left alone. If it does not always and at every turn resist every change, it does put a heavy burden upon every changer.

A thought much in any Presidential mind, when it plays upon the west wing of the Capital, has to do with prima donnas, ninety-six of them, holding at any moment God only knows what purposes and motivations and filled with God knows how many latent and hidden difficulties for a man trying to do a job.

The executive approach to the Institution, in consequence, often is as gingerly as that of a sentry in a lately occupied area. Two languages are involved in the relationship.

There is good reason for this, for it must be said that it

9

is possible to offend the Senate in odd and unexpected ways. No skin in all the world is more easily abraded than the Senatorial skin.

Once, for an illustration, the Attorney General of the United States, Herbert Brownell, Jr., was condemned to the pit of Senatorial displeasure for daring to permit his department, which undoubtedly has the function to advise upon legal matters, to prepare a memorandum raising certain questions about a variation of a proposed Amendment to the Constitution to limit the treaty-making powers of the Presidency.

The incident struck the then Dean of the Senate, Mr. George of Georgia, as intolerable. It was his conclusion, expressed in the tragically wounded tones of which his majestic voice was capable, that Brownell was "a very *odd* Attorney General" and worse still, that his offensive paper had undoubtedly been written by "some cloik" (clerk) in the Justice Department.

The whole of the Senate, on whatever side of the issue that had provoked it all, at once concurred with Mr. George that it had heard quite enough from Mr. Brownell—or his cloik.

There was more to the incident than that the Attorney General had picked the wrong day to confront the wrong man with his arguments. There was the important underlying fact that here the Institution felt itself to be functioning on the lonely plateau of one of its highest functions, the care and shaping of the Constitution of the United States. This, in its view, was no place for the Executive.

Still, it *is* possible, in theory anyway, for the President to get along with the Senate, much or some of the time, though it is a difficult business. First of all, it is necessary to know the inner tone of the place and to be able to sense what cannot be grasped. "If you can't smell a feeling," says Senator Lyndon Johnson of Texas, "you are no kind of a politician."

Then it is necessary to approach the place with a blend of confidence and of deference, of assertiveness and of care. The agent of the Executive must (or ought to) come forward prepared to yield much but to hold on to the bitter end to the core of his principle and purpose. He must make clear, at once, the permissible area for bargaining and the area that is out of bounds for compromise. But he must do all this subtly, neither belligerently nor fearfully, for Senators react with anger to the one and with contempt toward the other.

Much of the political story of the Republic is the story of intermittent contest between the Senate and the Presidency. "Strong" Presidents who have also been aggressive Presidents have, particularly since the nineteenth century, when Andrew Jackson proclaimed the sovereignty of the Executive, fought bitterly with the Institution. Theodore Roosevelt, Wilson, Franklin Roosevelt and Truman, all these are other ready examples. Power has been the

11

obvious prize; but at war, too, have been the present and future, as exemplified by the White House, and the past, as defended by the Senate. The one, the Presidency, has generally sought the expansion of quantitative democracy. The other, the Senate, has nearly always sought the preservation of a qualified and qualitative democracy. To it the movement of time is of time upon a belt; the yesterday that has just gone is just arriving. This is a body that never wholly changes and never quite dies. This is a "continuing body," where it is actually harder to change a rule than to vote to take a country to war. To such a body, where the national past and the national future meet and soundlessly merge—to such a body who and what, after all, is a mere transient President of the United States? These narrow little Senate seats, almost childish in their fragile simplicity of design, they have been there for a century and three quarters and more.

II

THE SENATE

AND THE SMALLNESS

THE SENATE of the United States has ever been bloodlessly and blandly at war with some of the main notions—call them concepts or call them folk myths—of the United States. The

13

country has long valued bigness as an end in itself—and in the jeers at the State of Texas, where the ideal of bigness *does* take on an uncomfortably sacramental quality, the perceptive ear will detect not only the expression of a moral judgment but also the hint of unexpressed envy.

The country has long valued homogeneity; and indeed a pretty good case could be made that increasingly it values conformity or, perhaps, rather a tiered series of conformities, where everyone has his proper place while tirelessly working to ascend to the tier just above. Expressed in material terms, the unskilled workman has, let us say, his much used Plymouth; the skilled has his new Ford; the foreman his De Soto; the insurance broker his Chrysler or Buick and his membership in the new golf club; the business executive his Cadillac and his older golf club; the third-generation rich man or well-to-do intellectual his Jaguar and hi-fi (no television set here).

And the country has long valued, or at least paid its highest lip service to, an idea of democracy largely expressed in mere numerical terms—that is, the terms of bigness. There seems little doubt that to most of the citizens of the United States the proper *definition* of democracy—one does not here necessarily mean the *practice* of democracy—would closely resemble the findings of a gigantic Gallup poll. The God, politically, is the Majority, making, *without restraint*, the ultimate decisions.

Everywhere, almost, is the goal of bigness. The President

of the United States is in effect elected by the bigness, by the majority. Even the vestigial electoral college system, by which it is conceivable that a minority President might be chosen, is under very heavy attack and probably needs only a small final push—say the actual election of a Presidential candidate who did not carry the popular majority—to be thrust from its old place in the Constitution.

Big Business, Big Labor, Big Farmers, Big Schools, Big Newspapers and Magazines, all these typify the common American scene.

But in the Senate it is the jewel in the cask, it is contraction and not expansion, that is held most dear.

Indeed, this Institution came upon the scene to check Bigness, a Big Federal Government, the Big States, the Big Parties—and even the Big Majority. A Borah from the remote, ill-populated and then utterly insular State of Idaho once held a commanding power over the foreign affairs of the United States before which even Presidents had to pause. (Secretaries of State counted hardly at all.) It was perhaps not a wisely executed power but the point of the moment is that it was a *Senatorial* power based ostensibly on the suffrage of a handful of miners and sheepherders and the like whose total assets would hardly have made a noticeable entry in the daily deposits of a single New York bank. The Borah voters would have been lost in any small part of any one of the five boroughs of New York City; they were important to Borah, but Borah was important not

15

because of Idaho but because of what the Senate is.

For Borah was more influential, in his day and in his field, than all the Senators from New York, New Jersey and Pennsylvania and half a dozen other States put together— and the whole of the House of Representatives. The Foreign Office of the United States was very often in his hat and, the Senate being what it is, only defeat or death, and in his case it was death, could have taken it from him. His mandate was from the Senate Foreign Relations Committee, of which he was so long the chairman.

Then, there was Pat McCarran, whose last re-election to the Senate was ordained by the sovereign ballots of 35,829 Nevadans while 3,853,934 New Yorkers were returning Senator Irving M. Ives. (The population of Nevada in 1950 was 160,083; that of New York, 14,830,192.)

McCarran largely made the immigration policy of the United States, constricting, as he did so, the traditional haven so eloquently described in stone on the Statue of Liberty. McCarran kept in some degree of complaisance and terror the Department of Justice of the United States in more than one administration. McCarran, through his chairmanship of the Senate Judiciary Committee, which must approve all nominees to the high Federal bench, unquestionably had a hand in shaping the tone of the judiciary of the United States. McCarran, through his chairmanship of the Senate Subcommittee on Internal Security, an offspring of the Committee on the Judiciary, for years largely and personally

16

decreed what was to be considered loyal and faithful and unsubversive conduct in the United States.

Then there was Senator George Norris. Nebraska, his state, is, of course, no Idaho, as it is no Nevada. Still, thriving though it is and far from negligible though it is in population, it is hardly a Pennsylvania or a California in terms of the numbers, the Bigness.

But Norris for years—and very important years they were, at a time when the Depression was turning some men off into very odd and ugly political searches—lifted a powerful voice for clean liberalism in the only chamber where there could have been a Norris at all. Such a man was he that when Franklin Roosevelt went about forming the Tennessee Valley Authority he sat in an automobile overlooking that then ravaged river, put his arm about this Senator from Nebraska and, in the very presence of the then senior Senator from Tennessee, Kenneth McKellar, said softly:

"George, I want *you* to introduce the bill." (This I was told, with a certain bitterness, by old Senator McKellar himself.)

It can be argued that Borah had too much power for the good of the country; it can hardly be denied that this was the case as to McCarran. But would many now argue—even those wholly opposed to his political notions—that it is a bad thing that there is such a place as the Senate to nurture the peculiar talents of so dedicated a man as George Norris?

Conscious though one is of the abuse of Senatorial power, one glories nevertheless in the circumstance that there is

17

such a place, where Big Senators may rise and flourish from Small States.

The Senate, though the Senate of the United States, is in fact the Senate of the States, so that never here will the cloud of uniformism roll over the sun of the individual and the minority. The Bigness, the majority, may have its President. But the contrary, the non-conforming—even the prejudiced and the unalterably wrongheaded—they, too, have their place and their representation.

For the Institution protects and expresses that last, true heart of the democratic theory, the triumphant distinction and oneness of the individual and of the little State, the infinite variety in each of which is the juice of national life.

It is perhaps often forgotten that the democratic ideal is *not* all majority; that, indeed, at its most exquisite moments the ideal is not for the majority of all but actually for the minority of one. The practice of majority rule, *in some things,* is properly revered. But who would surrender the safeguard that *one* of twelve jurors may protect the *one* man in the dock? The right of Congress by majority vote to make the laws is admirably planned. But twenty Congresses supported in their actions by 90 per cent of the American people will twenty times make their enactments and twenty times have them thrust aside if they seek to abridge the right of a single American to publish his little paper, however odd, or take up his little religion, however strange.

The Senate, therefore, may be seen as a uniquely *Consti-*

tutional place in that it is here, and here alone, outside the courts—to which access is not always easy—that the minority will again and again be defended against the majority's most passionate will.

This is a large part of the whole meaning of the Institution. Deliberately it puts Rhode Island, in terms of power, on equal footing with Illinois. Deliberately, by its tradition and practice of substantially unlimited debate, it rarely closes the door to any idea, however wrong, until all that can possibly be said has been said, and said again. The price, sometimes, is high. The time killing, sometimes, seems intolerable and dangerous. The license, sometimes, seems endless: but he who silences the cruel and irresponsible man today must first recall that the brave and lonely man may in the same way be silenced tomorrow.

And those who mock the Institution, and demand of it "speed" and yet more speed and "efficiency" and yet more efficiency, might remember that there is altogether a good deal of both at present in American life. For illustration, those who denounce the filibuster against, say, the compulsory civil rights program, might recall that the weapon has more than one blade and that today's pleading minority could become tomorrow's arrogant majority. They might recall, too, that the techniques of communication, and with them the drenching power of propaganda, have vastly risen in our time when the gaunt aerials thrust upward all across the land. They might recall that the public is not *always* right all at once and that it is perhaps not too bad to have *one* place in which matters can be examined at leisure, even if a leisure uncomfortably prolonged.

They might be interested, for example, in the estimate of responsible politicians that at one time in our history—specifically in the 1920's—the Ku Klux Klan held political control, overt or in shadow, in as many as twenty-six American States. The point arises that this conceivably could have meant fifty-two pro-Klan Senators out of a total of ninety-six. The question follows thus: Would it really be wise to alter the Senate rules so that a simple majority could halt a filibuster by voting cloture, instead of a two-thirds majority of all Senators, or sixty-four, as at present? It is a rhetorical question in one sense, and an academic one in another: The Senate, depend upon it, will make no such alteration.

Indeed, the degree of Senate intolerance toward proposals to change its way of life is matched only by the degree of Senatorial tolerance of the first necessity of the American political method—the necessity to compromise the demands of the sections and of the interests.

The body pre-eminently is an amalgam of the States, a national institution only in the sense that it is not possible to avoid having the parts sum up to the whole, and thus to a considerable degree it is an amalgam of the sections. It was the Senate that informed Calhoun of South Carolina, an eminent Senator of parts, to lay down the most classical, and still the most irreplaceable dictum of our practical politics. This was the Doctrine of the Concurrent Majority, in which Calhoun postulated that this was necessarily a country of so many harsh and fundamental divisions that the central demand of the art of politics was to accommodate and merge and thus ameliorate the divergencies lest they become inflamed beyond cure.

The Senate was the ideal home for this philosophy (which probably has kept this a two-party rather than a multi-party nation) since accommodation and compromise lie at the deepest root of its tradition. Calhoun was only stating what was, in the Institution, already a great fact of its life.

The fundamental meaning of the Doctrine of the Concurrent Majority was, and is, that to pursue political differences to ultimates in the mortal, Balkan sense is not only fruitless but extremely unwise. In other words, it was not, and is not, a tenable act to press upon any minority, sectional or otherwise, policies or laws that are quite literally intolerable, though of course care must be taken not to equate the truly intolerable with the merely repugnant. This concept and practice, too, upon examination will be seen to fall very neatly into the great spirit of the Constitution. That spirit was not to form a YMCA of brothers linking arms and chanting glad hosannas of mutual love but simply to find and fix upon a reasonable *modus vivendi* by which the differing States and peoples could live as well as might be in the Federated life.

It might be urged that Calhoun's doctrine fared ill in the

21

debates that preceded the War Between the States and far worse while the guns still were firing from Vicksburg to Gettysburg, and afterward in the Reconstruction. But then it would have to be added that the doctrine plainly lay at the bottom of the wise and sensible policy of the first and greatest Republican President, Mr. Lincoln; that had it been followed during the Reconstruction this would be a far different country, without, perhaps a single Bilbo on its political roster, and that the doctrine has on the whole gone on gathering power and validity ever since.

It has done this not only because it is a wise policy but because, especially considering that there *is* a Senate, it is a most necessary one. When numerical considerations were largely discarded in forming the place, the frame of reference had to become qualitative. Once it became qualitative, *accommodation* had to guide the course of affairs. There is not much, perhaps, by urban Eastern standards to the economy of the State of Wyoming. It is nevertheless of the most poignant concern to Wyoming and to Senator Joseph C. O'Mahoney of that State. And since O'Mahoney has as much right, and as much forum space, as a Senator from, for example, Michigan, with its fabulous Willow Runs and all that, what must now ensue?

Why, reasonable men, unable simply to engulf the O'Mahoneys with their votes, as they well might in the House of Representatives and as they easily could in any nationwide election, must find a way to deal with them. This leads, of course, to what is called logrolling. And logrolling has been given an evil sound by cliché and custom—sometimes by men who see no special evil in the accommodations that go on in collective bargaining between industries and labor.

This is the sure Senate path, rarely departed from, this path of negotiation and compromise, for to take another path for long would mean the end of the whole numerically unrepresentative basis of the Senate itself. Parenthetically, the real and earnest difficulty about adding States to the Union has been a good deal more subtle than the obvious reasons. These obvious reasons have involved the fact that Hawaii, for example, would presumably be Republican and Alaska, for example, would presumably be Democratic and neither party has been anxious to present the other with two additional Senate seats. They also have involved a conservative fear of the power of union labor in Hawaii; the simple fact of non-contiguity as to both Territories, and the not very pretty but quite plain fact that some Senators are afraid of the color of some of the people of Hawaii.

Down beneath, however, the basic trouble has been a general lack of Senate inclination to add new fellows to the Club and new seats to the Senate. Small-State Senators glory in the genial imbalance that puts them and their States where they are in the Institution; but they do not rush headlong to extend the imbalance. Large-State Senators, though satisfied with things as they are, nevertheless are not overly inclined to give an Alaskan handful and a Hawaiian double handful

23

the generous privileges of the place already extended to such States as New Mexico.

(I once asked members of the most conservative business-men's club in Tennessee what they thought of the Tennessee Valley Authority. The consensus was that it was fine—*where it was*—but that it would be monstrous and entirely out of the question to reproduce it elsewhere.)

At all events, the Doctrine of the Concurrent Majority is as much a part of the Senate as is the daily journal that is so rarely read. The consequence is that this is, oddly, not really a very partisan place, incredible though this statement may seem, as partisanship is normally understood—that is, as bitter and unending friction between two *parties*. Here, the friction is more commonly ideological—and even per-sonal—than partisan, and most of it is in one way or another sectionally based or sectionally influenced. (Calhoun knew that, in his day, and took great care that the thing should not get out of bounds).

In the ten years or so that I have watched the Institution at close hand it has seemed to me that centrifugal force has on the whole tended progressively to weaken and that the general movement has been one of inwardness. The political center has thus greatly enlarged and the extreme wings have greatly shrunk.

This has no doubt been so in part for two reasons: There has been in this period no domestic economic cataclysm to worsen the ever-present sectional economic rivalries, and the greatest foreign crisis since the Second World War, the Korean action, was in fact generally popular and generally supported in the Senate during the time that counted most, no matter how many hard words were said about it later.

The inherent cause, however, has been that to a very considerable degree the Senate's privately distilled Doctrine of the Concurrent Majority of late has been to a degree adopted, whether for long or short term, by the country itself. The election of President Eisenhower in 1952 meant many things, of course, but one of the things it meant was that the country had gone in for the policy of accommodation and amelioration, whether consciously or not.

In a narrower sense, but a more important sense to the purpose here at hand, it reflected the decision of the Republican party, taken at the 1952 Chicago convention in the rejection of Senator Taft and the elevation of General Eisenhower, to cease being, nationally, quite so Republican.

This decision, though not actually then pleasing to a majority of the Republicans in the Senate, had, for all that, the inevitable effect of turning the subsequent Senate leadership toward the concept of accommodation. The years since have on the whole been fairly amicable Senate years; the outsider would be surprised to know how genuinely fond of each other have been the two recent party leaders, the sober, muscular Senator Knowland of California for the Republicans and the thinner, more intense and yet more casual Senator Johnson of Texas for the Democrats.

One wishes to avoid any slightest overstatement of the case. All the same, it might even be said that the Senatorial way—the small, outmoded way, so to speak—has in recent years rather well pervaded the practical functioning of the whole Government of the United States, even though some manifestations of that Government have been profoundly un-Senatorial.

THE WAY

IT ALL STARTED

THE WORD Senate means literally an assembly of old men or elders—a rather apt description of a body that in the late Eighty-fourth Congress held fifteen members of more than seventy years of age (with six of them, indeed, over seventy-five years of age) and a vast majority who had passed the sixtieth birthday.

The term comes from ancient Rome, where the Senate originally was the supreme council of state, made up initially of a hundred nobles. The council, fittingly enough, began with only advisory powers but expanded its functions until at last it was making administrative decisions and laws.

The general sense of upheaval that accompanied the American Revolution changed, fleetingly or not, a great many things but some things were left profoundly unchanged—as some are today. There was a deep-seated colonial notion that while it would hardly do in the borning Republic to adopt the prevailing standard of admission to the House of Lords (there being, for one thing, no hereditary nobles hereabouts) it was most essential to set up an upper legislative chamber to check or refine the inevitable excesses of popular government and in general to speak for the educated, the well-born and the well-to-do.

While anyone old enough to remember the vast pother accompanying the repeal of the Prohibition Amendment would hardly believe it, the fact is that the pre-Federal issue of the proper composition and nature of the American Senate was one of the greatest and most acute Constitutional issues in the life of the country.

The indisputably British semi-character of the Institution that emerged—for all the fact that it was Roman in nomenclature, far more than merely British, and a unique governmental instrument carrying more than legislative powers— cannot be doubted now any more than then. (It is diverting at times to reflect from the gallery that when Senator Jenner of Indiana, for example, arises to disclose a suspicion of the British so deep and active as to amount almost to phobia, he himself was never more British in his life than in this act and that he speaks from a forum raised up by men representing the British race.)

For the first Senate, in all that it was and had, was the expression—though by unexampled extension—of a British point of view and a British habit of life. It was formed of a great compromise that never was in fact a compromise at all. It was an effort, so typically made up of the quality of muddle-through, to set up a virile parliamentary power in a Government that was not to be, in the British sense, a parliamentary government at all.

Nevertheless, there was for all this no really "serviceable model," as was more than once painfully observed in the Federal Convention of 1787, and the going was very sticky at times.

The Convention having fairly readily agreed that the national legislature ought to have two branches, there immediately arose the historic argument of the claims of the many relative to the claims of the few. The small States quite well knew their minds, and their delegations in some cases had explicit and fixed orders from home. For example, the men from Delaware, the very model of the small State, had come armed with instructions that "in determining Questions in the United States in Congress assembled, each State shall have one Vote."

Upon this rock stood all the small—that nothing could cause them to agree to anything but precisely equal State sovereignty.

All the same the delegations from the large States at length won the day so far as the House of Representatives, the lower chamber, was concerned, and at once the small fixed their hopes where always they had and have really been— upon the Institution that in nearly two centuries since has never really failed them in crisis. Proportional representation was adopted for the House, and the Convention now moved to the climactic business of creating the Senate. As it did so the small States began marshalling the last of their resources. They scurried about to require the immediate attendance of all the then absent delegations that had been assigned to represent such States.

Ellsworth of Connecticut now proposed that each State should have "an equal vote in the second branch" and for ten days there was bitter debate on the motion. There was talk that it might become necessary, in order to avoid the total rule of the smaller States, for Pennsylvania to swallow up Delaware and for New Jersey to be split between New York and Pennsylvania. There was even some resonant suggestion of how fine an arbiter was the sword.

At length, there came the "Great Compromise" that was in a real sense no compromise at all since it reflected a complete victory for the concept of a numerically unrepresentative Institution. The bone thrown to the majority rulers was that though the principle of the "equal voice" for the States would obtain in the Senate, the House membership would be based on population.

The principle having thus been established, it remained to dispose of some very important details. How should members of "the second branch," the Senate, be chosen? Some proposed that they be appointed by the President, a recommendation that got almost no consideration at all. There was even some vague talk (which did not materialize into action for a century and a quarter) that Senators be *popularly elected.*

This was altogether too much for the Convention, which seems to have regarded the advocate of this extraordinary course, James Wilson, as a most curious and quite possibly a very dangerous man. Sherman thought the people had altogether too much to do with the Government as it was. Gerry considered "the People" as being "chiefly composed of the landed interest" and thought that an all-popular Congress elected by such "people" would put the commercial, or non-agrarian, interests of the country on a thin diet indeed. (Gerry was partly right, whether or not for the right reason: The farmers still have a wholly disproportionate weight in the Senate of the United States.)

31

There was much talk, apparently shocking to no one at the Convention, to the effect that the voters were filled here and there with Heaven knew what bizarre notions, some of them even believing in the desirability of paper money. Obviously, the dominant Convention opinion was that when it came to the things and the organisms that mattered (and from even its pre-natal days the Senate very much *mattered*) there should be a policy, as Madison put it, "of refining the popular appointment by successive filtrations."

There was a proposal—this by Hamilton, whose massive and gloomy distrust of the people seems never to have wavered—for the selection of Senators in each State by six to twelve electors who themselves would be chosen by the large landholders. "Filtrations" indeed! The word was Madison's, but it remained for Hamilton to filter even that word.

Then, there was the suggestion that the Senate be made up of members to be chosen by the first branch, the House of Representatives. This went down very poorly. And it is possible even today to suspect that some atavistic Senate memory of this shocking presumption, this incredible proposal to put the House into the governance of Senate affairs, is involved in the tireless campaign of the Institution to keep "the lower body" in its place.

Is it not possible that something of this sort is remotely at the back of the obvious pleasure felt by a Senate Democratic leader such as Senator Lyndon Johnson of Texas when his mentor and lifelong friend, the Speaker of the House,

Sam Rayburn, calls upon *Johnson*, rather than the other way round?

At length it was fixed upon that the State Legislatures, which were then apparently in infinitely more agreeable odor than at present, should select two Senators from each State. James Wilson, who so long and so alone had urged the popular way, was disturbed and distressed.

He forecast, and it was with complete accuracy to the degree that he was talking about effects, that these totally different methods of selecting the membership of the two chambers would mean inherently different chambers between which there would be chronic disputation. This did not trouble the others. They wanted it that way, and that way it has largely been. What Wilson could not possibly foresee, in his jeremiads, was that even after the adoption in 1913 of the Seventeenth Amendment, which provided for the popular election of Senators, his case would be quite as good as it ever was.

For the Convention that settled all this settled other matters that for all time put upon the Senate the imprint of differentness. What was being created here was not merely a legislative instrument, however lofty, but an instrument with mixed functions in the executive and judicial as well as the legislative and investigative fields.

And it was so arranged that while the House of Representatives would be subject to total overturn every two years, and the Presidency every four, the Senate, as a Senate, could *never* be repudiated. It was fixed, through the staggered-term principle, so that only a third of the total membership would be up for re-election every two years. It is therefore literally not possible for the voters ever to get at anything approaching a majority of the members of the Institution at any one time.

It is in this light, the light of an organism having beginnings but never an end and holding a kind of limitless writ over the American life, that the Senate has one of its unique qualities.

For the Founders—incidentally having grandly cast aside as a mere mercantile question a proposal that the Senators be paid more than members of the House—now went forward to the business of adding superlatives of power to the place of pomp and of power that they were creating.

Very nearly given to the Senate was the power exclusively to make treaties, and not merely to advise and consent in their making, and to appoint "public ministers," and not merely to confirm these appointments.

Mr. George H. Haynes, upon whose monumental two-volume history, *The Senate of the United States*, I have most heavily and most gratefully leaned in these dealings with the past, notes that on August 6 the Convention's powerful Committee on Detail roundly proposed: "The Senate of the United States shall have power to make treaties, and to appoint Ambassadors and Judges of the Supreme Court."

It was argued that this extraordinary provision could permit the Senate to "sell the whole country by treaties" and oppositely that in this power of ultimate lawmaking the Senate ought to be the master and the President the mere agent—since the Senate alone represented the States whereas, by implication, the President represented merely the people.

In passing, Gouverneur Morris put in a thrust that has a perfect parallel in the efforts nearly two centuries later of Senator John W. Bricker of Ohio to limit the Presidential treaty-making power. Mr. Morris urged vainly, precisely as Senator Bricker was doing a good deal more recently in our history, an amendment stipulating that "no treaty shall be binding on the United States which is not ratified by law."

Wilson, the luckless, who quite clearly would never have made a good Senate man, bobbed up again to suggest that the House be brought into the treaty-making business. He failed signally again, and at last it was agreed that treaties must be made by the President with the advice and consent of the Senate and that they would not be ratified without the concurrence of two-thirds of those Senators voting.

Thus, the Institution was empowered in an unprecedented way to deal with foreign relations, not withstanding that the Constitution sought in the last analysis to leave these matters to the President. For whatever agency can define the terms of acceptability for a treaty can put the one partner to it, the American White House, under irresistible pressure to amend its whole design in negotiation. And it can put upon the other partner, the foreign chancellery, an enormous burden of good-will seeking. It can, in short, force alteration in the most basic relationships between this and other peoples.

Still, not all this was enough for the Founders, for the men who made the Senate. Having given it unspoken eminence over the House of Representatives, having given it protection from the people, a considerable degree of which still survives, what was next to do?

First, there was the matter of seeing to it that the Senate would have the power of immediate entry into the official Presidential household and into the Courts. Characteristically, it was again proposed that "the national legislature" —and one can easily guess whether in practice this would have meant primarily the House or primarily the Senate— should actually appoint the judiciary.

Objection was made that "numerous bodies" (for this read the House of Representatives) were not good at this sort of thing. Madison was, as he said, "rather inclined to give it [the appointing power] to the Senatorial branch," which was not so "numerous" as to be unworthy "to be confided in."

The Convention's Committee of the Whole, indeed, unanimously agreed that the Senate alone ought to choose the judges of the courts.

At this point, however, perhaps because all this was really getting a bit too thick even for the makers of the Senate, Massachusetts came forward to point out that for 140 years that Commonwealth had been well served through judicial appointments made by the Executive "by and with the advice and consent" of the Legislature.

Thus it finally fell out that to the Senate was given these incomparable rights: to accept or reject treaties; to accept or reject Presidential appointments both to the bench and to his own intimate Cabinet.

Then, as perquisite was piled upon perquisite for the Institution, there came what was in the sense of domestic power the most significant and the least-used of all.

The most influential of pre-Convention planning had envisaged the high judiciary as the proper place for trying impeachment actions, since these were after all bodies learned in the law and practiced in the judgment of men. Presently, however, there arose an obvious difficulty. If the Supreme Court should be set up as also the high court of impeachment, who was it that could try a justice if he fell into evil?

It was at length decided, and characteristically, as power gathered about the Institution, that while the House should be the body to bring impeachments, the Senate alone would have the ultimate right to try all impeachments, including the impeachment of any President of the United States.

37

"Has it [the Senate] not an authority over all the acts of the Executive?" asked Monroe. "What are the acts which the President can do without them?"

This, then, was the Institution as it evolved from the heads of the men of the Convention. It was, in theory, one part of one of the three branches of the Government. But, shaped and given life by the few and in the essentials doggedly non-representative of the many, where was its real field and what was its actual mandate?

It had been said, in the Constitution as a whole, that there were to be the three branches and, in substance, that each was to avoid trespass upon the others. But while the President was given no avenue to intrude upon the legislative part and, indeed, no avenue toward control of the judiciary except to make appointments that by life tenure made independent the appointee, what was now to be said for the Senate?

It had been given a moral primacy, at least, over the more popular branch of the legislature, the House, and in one matter an explicit primacy. The power to judge (the impeachment method is here recalled) is surely higher, is it not, than the power to accuse?

It had been given the sanction to hold to account, both before and during their accession to public place, the most important officials of the President's branch and of the judicial branch. These, though so infrequently employed, are far from negligible powers, as any Federal judge or Cabinet officer will know.

Finally, it had been given a distant dominion, immense for all its seemingly shadowy quality, over the conduct of the foreign affairs of this great new power arising in the West.

It is not surprising, then, that for the Senate nearly two hundred years of history may be as yesterday. It was only yesterday that the Convention placed in the Senate the power to remove the members of the Supreme Court of the United States—or a President. And it was only in a slightly less remote yesterday that the Senate would not let a President alter that court by addition.

It was only yesterday that the Convention considered giving total authority over treaties to the Institution. Is it any wonder that a President named Wilson had trouble with the treaty that was the League of Nations? That a President named Truman, and later a President named Eisenhower, were watched with such hawks' eyes from the Senate chamber in their approaches to Communist China? Is it any wonder even that a Senator named Bricker, considering the Institution in which he sits, came so very close a few years ago to restricting the treaty power?

He would have done it, too (as of course he or another might yet), but for another aspect of the Institution. This is the aspect that permits the ultimate minority—a single member, however junior—to taunt and to torture, gravely

39

to tutor and then to triumph over, the majority and the graybeards of the Senate. In 1954 such a Senator, Hennings of Missouri, with unanswerable logic in debate broke the Bricker amendment, in a body theretofore committed to it by two to one.

The bar associations, the patriotic societies, the letterwriters—few of these would listen to Hennings. But the Senate would, and did.

IV

THE PURSUIT

AND THE PERQUISITE

THE FIRST session of the Senate of the United States, which met in Federal Hall in New York on March 4, 1789, performed with the finest regard for the pattern that it was, all

41

unknowingly, setting with such aptness. Everything it did it was late in doing. And not one day had passed before there were strong indications, later materialized into the hard fact of history through one hundred and sixty-eight sessions of the Senate in eighty-four Congresses and many special sessions as well, that this Institution was not going to be in any great hurry in dealing with the public business.

Eligible to sit in the hall on opening day were in theory twenty-six Senators, two from each of the sovereign thirteen States. On hand were eight Senators but not on hand were ten others who had been duly and properly elected. (The eight additional ones were not truly chargeable with tardiness since they were still in process of selection by the legislatures of their States.)

The eight men met daily for a week only to adjourn; they were having an occupational Senate trouble, the frequent absence of a quorum. At length they prepared a letter to the absent ten, appealing to them "that you will be so obliging as to attend as soon as possible." This appeal had to be followed by another and more urgent one and the first quorum—that is, a majority by one of the total membership —was not obtained until April 6.

The House of Representatives, for its part, was up and doing, as always since it has been. That body by April 1 had chosen its Speaker and all its other officials and was just about to open debate on the question of what the tariff should be upon rum and molasses.

President Washington, like the Senate, was himself not rushing madly about. It was not until April 30, some two months after the appointed date for the inauguration of the new Government, that he took his oath of office and then went to the Senate chamber to deliver his inaugural address.

The members of the House of Representatives were on hand, but assembled in the Senate chamber. (In much more recent years Presidential addresses to joint sessions of Congress are delivered in the House, because this is the only chamber big enough to accommodate everybody. On these occasions, the Senators march across the Capitol more or less two by two, enter the House, look about doubtfully rather like dowager ladies finding themselves on lower Third Avenue in New York, and then gingerly take their places.)

The first Senate that heard the first Presidential speech of George Washington—and found, by the way, no difficulty in restraining its enthusiasm—was in many important details very similar to the Senate of today. Nineteen of the twenty-six members had served either in the Continental Congress or the Congress of the Confederation; many present Senators are old House of Representatives men.

Sixteen of the original twenty-six were lawyers or had legal training—and the law still is the dominant profession in the Senate of today. Nearly all of the twenty-six were substantial men of property; and that is true of a majority of the ninety-six of today. In the Senate of the Eighty-fourth Congress in 1956 there were fourteen members running

43

from extremely well-to-do to rich. (Five of the six who were *very* rich were Democrats, the supposed party of the poor; but this fact is not so odd as it sounds. Curiously enough, there is a perceptible tendency among the immensely wealthy as well as the angrily needy to "go Democratic"; much of the economic base of the Republican party is still typified by the small-town banker with one million, and not so much by the inheritors of old family fortunes running to many millions.)

And the Senators upon whom Washington gazed were, for the most part, profoundly "safe" men—not to mention men of fairly long-established records of fairly disinterested public service. This, too, is still largely true of Senators, however doubtful it may seem.

President Washington, who appears in this one regard to have been remarkably like a certain successor, also an ex-general who took the oath a hundred and sixty-four years later, set out at once to deal with the Institution in the greatest respect and with all punctilio. As the latter President, General Eisenhower, was especially careful to follow the precedents in Presidential-Senatorial relationships, the first President, General Washington, was especially careful in setting those precedents. "Many things which appear of little consequence in themselves and at the beginning," Washington observed, "may have great and durable consequences from their having been established at the commencement of a new general government."

Washington, having been formally called upon by a good

many members of the first Senate, at once set out to return these courtesies, as General Eisenhower so meticulously did in a sense in the round of breakfasts, luncheons and so on that he undertook with another Senate in 1953 and 1954.

Then, as now, the White House sought, however, to avoid indiscriminate hospitality to the Senate. And then, as now, the Senate was very much on its dignity, tending to regard any assiduous social Presidential attentions as an effort to undermine Senate independence and at the same time to resent as a sort of slur any Presidential inattention socially. Senator Maclay of Pennsylvania, who may confidently be regarded as one of the very first true "Senate men," was not to be gulled by Presidential receptions.

Of one of these he wrote of his fear "that from these small beginnings we shall follow on, nor cease, until we have reached the summit of court etiquette and all the frivolities, fopperies and expense practiced in European governments." Maclay nevertheless *went* to these dreadful affairs and on one occasion he complained in his diary of Presidential neglect at not being invited to more. "How unworthy of a great character is such littleness!" he observed.

Again, and here one can almost hear speaking a true "Senate man" of our time, say Senator Russell of Georgia, Maclay observed of President Washington: "He is but a man, but really a good one, and we can have nothing to fear from him, *but much from the precedents which he may establish.*"

Fear of the "precedents" that other governmental powers,

45

notably the Presidency, "may establish" is as much a part of the Senate as is its fondness for unhurried, unlimited debate.

Indeed, this first Senate soon showed the first President who it was who was to make the precedents and to have the perquisites, and this is about the way it has been ever since. It found itself quite unable to resist retorting to the President's first address. The Senate committee appointed to draft a reply came in with a report that amounted to a series of suggestions to the President; the same thing is done now by the issuance of statements or through individual speeches "reacting" to Presidential speeches.

Other and far more significant precedent-setting by the Senate soon followed. The Institution, after a good deal of talking, voted to confirm the first appointment sent up by the President, that of William Short to be Chargé to the Court of France in the temporary absence of the American Minister, Mr. Jefferson.

On the very next such occasion, however, it rebuffed the President—and recall that he was a very *popular* President—over an appointment that had no interest whatever to the people of the United States in general. Along with about a hundred other routine selections President Washington had asked the Senate to "advise and consent" to the nomination of Benjamin Fishbourne to be Naval Officer at the port of Savannah.

Word got about the Senate that one or perhaps both of

the Georgia Senators did not care for Mr. Fishbourne; and that was that. His nomination was rejected and there was established the precedent of "Senatorial courtesy" by which, for generations, the Senate has declined to confirm any appointee for lesser office who may be "personally obnoxious" to one or both of the Senators from the appointee's home State.

The more important effect was to put the Presidency on notice, thus so very early in the game, that the Institution (a) would infallibly look out for its own and (b) would interpret very liberally the power to "advise and consent," both here and in far more significant matters, such as treaties.

"Permit me to submit to your consideration," Washington then tartly told the Senate by letter, "whether on occasions when the propriety of nominations appears questionable to you, it would not be expedient to communicate that circumstance to me, and thereby avail yourselves of the information which led me to make them, and which I would with pleasure lay before you."

Or, in effect: Before you reject another of my nominations, ought you not to have some more or less objective ground for your action?

All this did not deeply move the Senate, which stood silent while, on August 7, 1789, the President withdrew the Fishbourn nomination and sent up another in its place. (In July, 1955, another President, Eisenhower, withdrew his nomination of Allen Whitfield of Iowa to be a member of the Atomic

Energy Commission. Whitfield had not been *rejected* in the Senate; his nomination had only been pointedly held up.

The Institution had not found it "expedient to communicate" its objections to Mr. Eisenhower; but these objections had found a channel to him just as the objections of August, 1789, had somehow reached Mr. Washington. Formal communication had still, after the lapse of many decades, somehow not been arranged by the Senate in these matters.)

But the Senate, having made the precedent in order to affirm and consolidate its power in this regard, now set off upon larger, and then far larger, affairs. Some of its powerful members raised the point that the Institution inherently had the right not merely to veto Presidential appointments but to veto Presidential removals of men from administrative office. Here was a great to-do indeed, though study of that period rather indicates that in this case Senatorial ambition was not really aflame and that Senatorial purposes were perhaps rather more to test the ground with the Executive, at the beginning of a tug for position and perquisite that has not abated through all the years, than to win a specific point.

At any rate, the debate was satisfyingly full—full of very large points and of those very fine points that the Senate so loves—and the outcome was a near thing. On the decisive vote, on the precise question whether the Senate should not require the approval of the Institution of any Presidential ouster of any man heading the Department of Foreign Affairs then in creation, the result was a tie. Vice-President

Adams, who seems never to have tired in his constancy to uphold Presidential office at every possible turn, joyfully broke the tie in favor of unrestricted Executive power in this field.

The result of the business nevertheless was again strongly to assert the claims of the Senate, which have never been unduly modest, while yet more important designs were afoot. These designs involved the vital area of treaties. President Washington, still feeling his way along but now showing a good deal more resolution than he had a few months before, had it in mind that while usually he might send treaty questions to the Institution in writing there would be times when oral communication was "indisputably necessary."

Accordingly, on August 22, 1789, he went to the Senate chamber at eleven-thirty o'clock in the morning to "advise with them on the terms of the treaty to be negotiated with the Southern Indians." He had perhaps decided on this dramatic, and at the same time informally friendly, method of approach because earlier it had required six weeks to obtain Senate consent to a routine consular treaty with France and three or four months to obtain action on pacts with some of the Indians in the North and Northwest. What the President intended, in short, was as politely as possible to prod the Institution—an enterprise into which so many Chief Executives have since cheerfully entered and sorrowfully withdrawn.

Washington took with him his Secretary of War, General

Knox. The Vice-President, Adams, loyally—and hurriedly—
read to the Senators the provisions of the treaty that the
President was proposing. At the end of each provision, Adams
inquired hopefully of the Senate: "Do you advise and consent. . . ?" Each time there was only thick silence. General
Knox produced some documents, but nobody paid any attention to them or to *him*. The President, so runs one account,
took on a look of "stern displeasure" that nothing at all of a
constructive nature seemed to be happening.

Senator Robert Morris of Pennsylvania for the moment
broke this somewhat icy deadlock—a President determined
on action and a Senate determined not to be rushed or over-
borne by the commanding presence of the visitor—by moving that the whole business be sent to committee.

A Sunday intervened and when on Monday President
Washington returned to the Senate, having earlier been
overheard to say that he would "be damned if he ever went
there again," he was in a contemporary account, now "placid
and serene and manifested a spirit of accommodation." As
he sat there the Institution rewrote his treaty before his eyes.

He never again went back there, with or without his ad-
ministrative experts, on treaty business, nor did any other
President of the United States until, 130 years afterward,
Woodrow Wilson went to the Senate to lay before it the
Treaty of Versailles.

Washington, for his part, had learned a great lesson. This
was that the Institution is a jealously *small* place, in the last

analysis really willing to admit and to listen only to its own, and that it reckons its collective wisdom in foreign affairs to be far greater than that of any Executive.

The first President thereafter put in writing all his proposals concerning treaties, expressing them, moreover, in deferential and conciliatory language, and quite often asked Senate opinion and explicit Senate recommendations even before beginning negotiations with other powers.

Harry S. Truman, whose sense of history is far more acute than many suppose, did the same thing when, with the Republicans in command of the Senate in the Eightieth Congress, he set out upon one of the great enterprises of American history. At the onset, in 1948, of the cold war, he reached the grave conclusion that the whole world balance was shifting and that the United Nations while a great instrument was not now enough.

He determined upon a project to bring the Atlantic free world together, to engage the United States in the first peacetime military alliance it had ever known, to accomplish this without breaking up the United Nations and in the teeth of an opposition Congress.

Mr. Truman did what Washington so long before had learned to do. He and Robert Lovett had first interested the Senate, and in practice at this period this meant the late Republican Senator from Michigan, Arthur Vandenberg, in the design. Vandenberg in due course brought from the Senate Foreign Relations Committee "the Vandenberg Resolution." It was precursor to the North Atlantic Treaty Organization, the final negotiation of which the Truman Administration now set off upon with all speed.

Here was no intrusion upon the Institution; here was deference and conciliation—and success. To have put such a proposal personally and directly before the Senate, as Washington had tried to do in connection with the Southern Indians, would have been fatal. To have embarked upon it without *indirectly* notifying the Senate, and engaging the good will of its senior persons, would have been silly.

What was done here was done the Senate way, and the consequence was implicitly to commit the leaders of the Institution before the rank and file was fully aware of what was afoot. The vast majority of the Senate fell quickly into line and the real opposition melted at the end to three most cautious Senators, Taft of Ohio, Watkins of Utah and Donnell of Missouri. Taft was . . . Taft; immensely and inherently suspicious of this as of nearly all other *Democratic* designs. Watkins was the kind of desperately earnest man who, in the argot of the writing profession, might be called an irreproachably correct comma chaser. Of Donnell, it was said, in exact truth, that he would not, in closing a letter to a friend, use the expression "My wife joins me in sending regards" until he had telephoned to inquire of Mrs. Donnell whether in actual truth she held such sentiments.

Again, the first crisis year in foreign policy for the Eisenhower Administration—the year 1955, with its threat of war over Formosa and then its offer of accommodation with the Russians at Geneva—went by as smoothly as it did in part because the claims to power laid down by the Senate nearly two centuries before were in every respect preserved and deferred to by the Executive. The way has been long, indeed, for the Institution, but time has not really passed there.

V

THE SENATE

AND THE RULES

THOUGH there is beyond doubt a great deal to be said for "progress," there *are* certain aspects of the progressive current American scene that do not necessarily enrich this best of all possible worlds. The America of the eighteenth century—and the Senate of this twentieth century no less than of the eighteenth—believed, ideally at least, in something called "playing the game," and that to play the game it is necessary to have, and on the whole to follow, certain rules. In many quarters today this expression, playing the game, may not too safely be used. There is, in widespread conviction, something stuffy, even something spinsterish, in it; and it is best left to the usage of vague ministers, seminarians, a few anglophilish professors of learning and, perhaps, the rather decayed Shakespearean actors.

So, too, with rules. From the teachers of "progressive" schools for the very young to such an unacademic personage as Mr. Leo Durocher there runs a common consent of thought that to obey mere *rules* is unduly harmful to the fine, free human personality and obstructive to its lawful ends. To Mr. Durocher, as a baseball manager, was attributed the most candid possible summation of the cult: "Nice guys finish last!"

The Senate, however, true here as elsewhere to what is now the minority, took the notion at the beginning and persists in it now that while rules of conduct are open to ridicule they are necessary all the same. To refrain from hitting one's grandmother with a spade involves a rule of personal conduct, and it is not a readily expendable rule no matter how much the act of self-abnegation represses the ego. To grant to one's opponent in high political discussion and maneuver each and all of the rights that one demands for himself—this is, uniquely in this country certainly, and perhaps in all the world, a Senate rule.

This is not, for example, really the attitude in the House of Representatives, where the will of the majority of the moment is absolute and where it is possible to require the House to act, even upon matters of great moment, in six or four or even two hours, as the hierarchs may decide. It is not really the attitude within the Executive Department—any Executive Department—where intellectual opposition to *any* Presidential course is given extremely small say. It is not, moreover, really the attitude in a Presidential election. The debates that go forward in Presidential campaigns are *on the whole* far less informed and far less tolerant than are great Senate debates.

This is not to say that there is not much of nonsense and worse in Senatorial discussion and it is not to deny that the political literature of the country has often been ennobled by striking and even imperishable passages uttered by Presidential candidates on the stump. What it *is* intended to say here is that in *no* struggle for the Presidency is there that tolerance of dissent, that *essential* search for approximate truth, that is found in major Senate debate.

The one, the Presidential campaign address, is at bottom pragmatic, involving at bottom simply a search for votes, entirely honorable as this pursuit may be. The other, the true Senate debate, at bottom is idealistic, no matter how many partisan and personal gains may at the same time be sought in it, involving at bottom an assembly and a synthesis of more nearly impersonal collective thought.

The one, the Presidential campaign address, necessarily begins and ends on a note of advocacy, advocacy of the speaker himself or of his ideas. The other, the Senate debate, indeed begins in a series of advocacies but ends upon the note not of advocacy but of collective judgment.

There could be no debate of this kind but for the fundamental fact that the Senate is the kind of place it is and but for the scarcely less requisite fact that the Senate has the rules that it has.

On the first day after the first session of the Institution had at last gathered up a quorum in 1789, a committee of five members, all lawyers, was selected to draw "rules for conducting the business of the Senate." On April 16 that year the committee brought in nineteen rules that for some seventeen decades have in fact governed. Though there have been many alterations and additions since, the whole body of the rules having reached forty in 1884 (and having stayed at forty in 1956), the original nineteen still express the spirit of the place. At the start, as now, the regulations for governing the House were more numerous, more explicit and more detailed.

The Institution for its part set out on the theory that it would always remain a relatively small body. It based all its rules upon the belief that natural courtesy and mutual deference among the members would be the best rule of all —as indeed it has been since the very old days when, sometimes, they gathered about the large fireplace in Federal Hall for their debates.

And since, unlike the House, the Senate is a continuing body, never ending and never wholly overturning from one Congress to the next, the Senate rules go on immutable from one Congress to another. It is not necessary to renew or continue them; there they stand as unshakable in fact, almost, as the Constitution itself.

All that is really necessary to know about them, in a wholly non-technical book such as this, is that not all of them together have one-tenth the force of simple tradition, the tradition that some things are done and some not done—or, if the expression may be forgiven, that in the Institution it is necessary to play the game. There is no purpose here in going into all of them; the gist of two will suffice. One of these forbids a Senator to call another Senator a liar or otherwise to question his honor. If he does so (as has sometimes happened in fact) a Senator may be made to interrupt his speech, take his seat and resume only "in order," that is, without repeating his violation. The other, the more or less famous Rule XXII, suggests an important change from the original cast of regulations—but the change is more superficial than real.

The Senate set out with no real limitation on how long a man might speak other than the limitation that his own conscience or sense of fitness might suggest. For several years, however, no doubt because of the influence of the British House of Commons, one school argued that it was possible in the Senate for debate to be halted by moving "the previous question," a parliamentary maneuver still widely used in the House of Representatives that halts discussion and brings matters to the voting point.

In 1806, in order to be absolutely certain about it, the Senate went vigorously on record for no limitation whatever. From 1806 to 1917, then, debate was absolutely free and unlimited except during the interregnum of the War Between the States. Even then, debate could be shut off only on war measures before the Senate.

In 1917, President Woodrow Wilson, angry because Senator Norris, Lane and others had killed by filibuster a wise and brave Administration bill to arm the merchant ships against the Germans, so denounced "the little group of wilful men" that the Institution took what was seemingly a most grave step.

It adopted Rule XXII, by which it was theoretically possible to choke off debate if two-thirds of those Senators present so decreed. Here, however, as so often elsewhere, the Senate advanced to the future only to retreat to the past. For the rule bore within itself the seeds of its own nullification. It was possible by two-thirds to halt debate on a "measure," but, as it turned out, not on a "motion." And there can be no "measure" before the Senate until first there is a "motion" to bring it up. Unlimited debate remained the Senate way.

In 1949, when President Truman was pressing hard for the compulsory civil rights program—to knock out the poll tax, racial discrimination in employment, and so on—liberal Senate forces (and some with designs other than purely liberal) attempted various devices to make the cloture, or the so-called "gag," more readily applicable. The theory was that if the filibuster could be broken, the civil rights program could be adopted, since a clear majority seemed to be in its favor.

The *facts* of the case, as I grasped them as a correspondent working close to the scene, were that while support of the Civil Rights Bill undoubtedly was professed by a majority, the true majority was made up between those openly opposed and those secretly opposed and filled with secret hope that somehow the issue could be put aside. The chief difference between the vehemently articulate Southern opposition to civil rights and a good deal of the rest of the Senate, in short, was the difference between harsh candor and no candor at all.

Intermixed in the whole business, moreover, was a not unnatural determination among the Republicans, who had so lately been cast out of power in Mr. Truman's incredible triumph at the polls in 1948, to do nothing to abate the internecine controversy among the Southern and Northern Democrats.

Here at issue was a great deal more than proper treatment for a minority, in this case primarily the Negro minority. Involved was the whole long concept, so closely held by the Senate generally since the outcome of the Federal Convention, of the ultimate supremacy of the individual State. Tragically involved was the sectional bitterness that had come, and had remained in part, from the War Between the States and the Reconstruction. And involved, moreover, was a historical dilemma for small-State Senators, however they might feel individually about compulsory civil rights as proposed by Mr. Truman.

For to promote the idea of cloture is, from the small-State point of view, to sharpen a dangerous weapon. It is, in the nature of the Senate, absolutely necessary for the small States to maintain the concept of the minority's veto power, having in mind that it is only within the Institution that this power can be asserted or maintained. (In the House, for example, New York State has forty-three voices to a single one for Nevada.)

It is only in the light of all these facts that the true nature of the Senate's debate of 1949 on Rule XXII can be understood. It is only in this same light that the contest can be seen as putting at stake a great deal more than a fusty exercise by a group of prolix old men.

The essential struggle lay between those who were determined to make the cloture truly effective and those determined that this should not be so. Long history has plainly indicated that the clamp upon debate simply will not in fact be pressed down, except possibly when the country is at war or in obvious and unarguable peril otherwise, where any *genuinely* adamant and substantial minority is prepared adamantly to resist. (The Calhoun Doctrine of the Concurrent Majority, of which mention has been made before this, stands in the way.)

It is equally clear beyond question to those who long have observed the Institution that where a powerful majority *really wants* a bill it will find a means to have its way, cloture or no cloture.

When, for example, the National Association for the Advancement of Colored People suspects that the combat intentions of some of its professed backers are less than desperately firm its suspicions are quite correct.

The rule existing in 1949—that two-thirds of those voting could put on the cloture but only on a "measure" and not on a "motion"—was, of course, in simple truth no rule at all. The retreat of 1917 before Wilson's sense of outrage had been, in the real sense, no retreat at all. Thus in 1949 the bottom purpose of the liberals—they were called this for convenience though some joining in efforts to harden the rule were hardly more liberal than William McKinley— was to make it possible to halt debate by simple majority. Their interrelated purpose was to do this to a "motion" as well as a "measure."

The Senate traditionalists—in both parties, it should be

realized—had for their purpose to do what had been done in 1917: to make it appear that they were not wholly uncompromising, but not to give up anything that fundamentally mattered.

This, indeed, was what was done at the end. It was agreed that hereafter the "motion" as well as the "measure" would fall under cloture's scope. But it was agreed also that thereafter no kind of cloture could be put on any future proposal to alter the rules, by any vote, or on any other matter short of the vote of two-thirds of the *entire* Senate, sixty-four members, instead of two-thirds of those voting, as before. The anti-filibuster people had won an ostensible battle only to lose a very real war. Cloture was in practical fact at least as far off as ever, and the Senate in plain fact retained what amounts to unlimited debate.

The liberals of 1949 had to make the most comfortable rationalization they could of the fact that considering the whole slope of Senate history the filibuster has been more often a *liberal* than a conservative device. Indeed, it had been the filibuster led in 1917 by the powerful Norris that had so provoked Wilson.

The conservatives, for their part, had to try to look as innocent as they could in the face of the undoubted fact that to a degree, and subject to the qualifications already noted here, they had taken action tending long to postpone the arrival of total equality of legislation for the Negroes. In protecting the *general* minority right in the deeply governmental sense—in making certain that the Institution would remain the minority's last forum—they had very clearly acted against the interests of a *particular* minority.

All this is a complicated business, indeed, full of the inescapable passions that touch alike upon racial and religious questions.

It is for the present perhaps enough to say only that not in all the great storms that have beset this Republic—not in the First World War, not in the Depression, not in the Second World War, not in the transient ascendancies of any and every White House—has the Senate, as a *whole Senate*, ever really given ground upon the issue of its rules.

Look at them as good or look at them as bad, the outstanding fact is that they remain, deeply unpopular though at times they may be. When, briefly, they were to some extent once abridged and breached, the body of the Institution was like a man with one leg. When the Southerners returned from the War Between the States the full operation of the old way was restored.

And thirty-six years before the rules had made the Senate a shelter to Woodrow Wilson's "little group of wilful men" he himself had written, in 1881, of these same rules:

"The Senate's opportunity for open and unrestricted discussion and its simple, comparatively unencumbered forms of procedure, unquestionably enable it to fulfill with very considerable success its high functions as a chamber of revision."

When Wilson spoke as he spoke in 1881 he was speaking as the academician that he was and coincidentally as a Southerner. But when he spoke as he spoke in 1917 he was speaking as a harassed President of the United States.

VI

OLD

SOUTHERN HOME

No MORE than twenty-two of the ninety-six members of the
Senate can ever be Southerners, for the great divide of
history and custom defines the true Southern territory as

the eleven States of the Old Confederacy. (In this connection the Border State people—the Marylanders, the Missourians, the Kentuckians, the Oklahomans, and the West Virginians —really need not apply.) Nevertheless, the place is, to most peculiar degree, a *Southern* Institution engrafted upon, or growing in at the heart of, this ostensibly national assembly of the sages.

So marked and so constant is this high degree of Southern dominion, in spirit or in fact in the varying times, that the Senate might be described without too much violence to fact as the South's unending revenge upon the North for Gettysburg.

The reasons for it all are varied and colorful, however regrettable the situation may be regarded. Within the Democratic party in the Senate, which since the end of the Reconstruction Era has on the whole held essentially an equivalent Senate power to that of the Republicans, the Southerners are almost always a bit on top of the game. Nearly always they are more powerful than their Northern colleagues of the same party. Moreover, and more importantly, in the final decisions of the Senate it is nearly always the Southerners whose influence is most pervasive and persuasive.

In the search for root causes it is necessary to go back to the beginning. The kind of Senate formed by the Federal Convention in the eighteenth century was peculiarly Southern both in flavor and structure. The great settlement made there, that providing for the equal voice of each State in the new Institution, expressed what later became the deepest and the most dangerous and the most bitterly held for all of all Southern political philosophies. It was a philosophy to be carried, in the nineteenth century, to the point of equating the principle of State sovereignty with the right to absolute State separatism, or, in a word, secession itself.

And it might well be recalled that the most influential of all the Founders of the Senate—Madison, Pinckney and others—were themselves men of Southern trait and Southern view. Finally, as far as the long past is concerned, the concept of the equal voice was accompanied by a quite unhidden concept not only that the Institution should *not* be popular but that its personnel should be aristocratic. This notion that Senators should also be aristocrats *is* dimming now in the South—and in the Senate—but no one should suppose that it has vanished altogether from either place.

The public's awareness of recent Southern politicians has been preoccupied with such spectacular vulgarians as Bilbo of Mississippi and Heflin of Alabama. It has perhaps been forgotten that such a blueblood as John Sharp Williams sat in the Senate from Mississippi ahead of Bilbo and that Alabama has known far more Bankheads and Lister Hills and Underwoods than it has known Heflins.

In the Senate of today the acceptable definitions of what is proper, there and elsewhere, are far more often made by Southerners, from their entrenched position of minority, than by all the rest of the place put together. No one would more quickly confirm this than would a Saltonstall of Massachusetts, who is so well-born that envy simply would not occur to him. The late Taft of Ohio, a member of one of the family dynasties of the country, instinctively recognized this when he first began to make his long series of accommodations with the Southern Democrats.

A sense of presence is somehow attached most of all to the Southerners. And to have presence in the Institution is useful beyond ready explanation, though to be effective it should be graciously used as, for illustration, it is used by Senator Byrd of Virginia, who employs his power by seeming not to employ it at all.

The breath of life of the Senate is, of course, continuity. And in the nature of the case continuity of service is the special property of the one-party-State Southerners. With continuity comes long experience. This is a body of subtle judgments and the most brilliant of arriving members will find that it requires years of learning to be able to be truly Senatorial.

And with experience, or merely with longevity in the Institution, comes the unique seniority power that goes with committee chairmanships. In the Eighty-fourth Congress *seven* of the nine truly powerful committees of the Senate had as their chairmen men from the Deep South and thus substantially in command of all legislation in these great committees. On the other two, Southerners were dominant on the Democratic side even though the actual chairman-ships were in non-Southern hands.

This disproportion of power will be seen as enormous when it is remembered that the whole lot of the Southerners make up less than one-third of the aggregate Senate.

How is this power, generally, used, and how is it made tolerable that the one-third should stand so astride the two-thirds? The question is answerable only in the character and special attitudes and attributes of the Southern Senator col-lectively considered.

He has, this archetype one describes here, both a soft voice and manner and underneath a flintlike determination to hang onto power and perquisite. Perpetually he fails ut-terly to dominate his *national* party at national conventions; when he has controlled some three hundred of the roughly twelve hundred votes cast in such a convention he has done about the best of which he is capable. But almost always he comes near to dominating his party in the Senate—and to a degree the Senate itself—precisely because of the qualities that make him a substantial failure outside the Institution.

While his party has in general maintained a liberal and forward-looking outlook since before the first World War, he has—as has the Senate itself—for the most part kept unchanged his dream of the past.

He has agreed to reforms only slowly and painfully and those who come to him calling for change must carry the most impressive of *bona fides*. He is not effective in any

71

forum (for example, the national convention) of sheer majority rule. For the most part, his whole political life (including his election and his re-elections to the Senate) is based upon the choice of *minorities* in position to control the actions of majorities.

He is pre-eminently *the* "Senate man" and this is his great home. It is not so much that he is so like the Institution as that the Institution is, in fundamentals, so like him. And his degree of at-homeness there, a chamber that he enters from his State with the quiet satisfaction of a man rising from his dinner table to stroll contentedly into his sitting room, is in every way unexampled. He loves what is for this country the center of unaltered traditions. He luxuriates in the dry, underplayed splendor of the place, and in the heavy power that so lightly and casually rests there. He venerates the only place in the country where the South did not lose the war.

Because his outmoded sense of the fitness of things is so great, he is, this archetype, generally more formally and more traditionally dressed than are the rest, and nearly always more archaically eloquent in debate. These qualities, however they may be looked upon "outside," are considered most admirable in the Senate—and they are much emulated.

Some Southerners do, of course, break the pattern and the mold. Byrd of Virginia, his frosty blue eyes twinkling, his apple cheeks glowing, speaks, oddly, with some of the tired, almost nasal quality of the Northerners, this conservative of conservatives. And to hear Holland of Florida is to be treated to an address that is half pedantic, much like an elderly professor, and half scholarly legalism, as though a Justice of the Supreme Court were tossing off, *in camera*, a few considered opinions to select members of the Bar of Philadelphia.

But the characteristic Southerner, what a mellifluous joy he is in debate! This man—George of Georgia, the late Senator Bailey from North Carolina, Stennis of Mississippi, any number of others from the South—will before he is through catch at the throat of the most cynical hearer.

He will begin softly, with wry self-deprecation, almost with an embarrassment of humility. He will say that he has, of course, only a very few words; all too well is he aware that it is not for *him* to intrude long upon the deliberations of his betters here.

He will find to have been very sound, indeed, nearly all that has been said before, by foe and friend. And then, as he goes along and the clock hands slip by, the tone, at first imperceptibly, will change. The voice toward which men had been leaning more or less intently, so low and calm was it, will begin to rise in volume and to fall in tone. And at the end it has become a commanding pipe organ, rolling and thundering out before the wicked, the foolish and the insensitive.

The Southerner will very much enjoy his performance, and so will those around him, but he finds himself considerably less than moved when non-Southern Senators attempt such tours de force.

All the same when these unhappy occasions do arise his sense of punctilio is so strong that, unlike many of the Northerners themselves, he will loyally remain in his seat to give attendance upon the effort, much as its shortcomings may pain him.

Because of his instinctive sympathy with the Institution and all that is in it, he is like a man who can put his hand instantly to any book in a cherished library. In consequence he is a past master of the precedents, the practices, and even the moods of the Senate and as a parliamentarian formidable in any debate or maneuver. He has "swallowed the rule book."

Though his sectional group is on some issues thoroughly divided, having its right and left wings on tax policy, housing and the like, there is in it at the last analysis a oneness found nowhere else in politics. And the Southerner in the Senate is also a Calhoun man to the bottom of his feet.

A Byrd of Virginia may look with troubled eyes upon the economic heresies of a Sparkman of Alabama, and a Sparkman may somberly return the gaze at what he thinks is the aura of parsimony rising about the seat of the senior Senator from Virginia. Nevertheless, when all is said and done, all are in the same clan, in a way that goes deeper than political ideas and even political conviction.

At the least suggestion of any slur upon any Southerner

74

in good grace (and to fall out of grace takes long and conscious effort) all will leap upon the assailant. A few years ago, for an illustration, Senator Humphrey of Minnesota rose to call into question one of Byrd's special projects, the Joint Committee on Reduction of Nonessential Federal Expenditures.

Humphrey attempted to suggest that this committee was not visibly doing very much and perhaps ought to be abolished. Any stranger present that day in the Senate galleries would have felt a pardonable and total mystification at what ensued. Before the unfortunate Mr. Humphrey (then new to the Senate) could have the slightest awareness of what was happening to him and why, he faced an outraged Senate. An anti-Humphrey demonstration raged for the better part of a whole day. It was led, of course, by the massed Southerners (not all of whom knew much or cared much about Mr. Byrd's joint committee). They, as always, recruited with them nearly all the Senate patriarchs of both parties.

When at length Senator Humphrey lurched dazed and wounded from the field of battle, all that was entirely clear was this, as he himself now wryly acknowledges: It had been a great mistake for him to challenge any part of the institutional activities of Senator Harry Flood Byrd of Virginia, a Southerner. True, Mr. Byrd might be thought by many of his own Southern colleagues to be in error in maintaining his joint committee. But that, surely, was hardly the point, was it?

Again, the Southern Senator maintains his own special code as to what is right and proper in the Senate and this he has not the slightest hesitation in articulating from time to time as the spirit moves him. The fact that he would react as though doused with acid if advised on *his* conduct by a non-Southerner is, as he sees it, hardly germane at all.

Still and all, he is a good fellow, the Southerner, and the Senate knows that without him it would not be the Institution at all. He is loyal and generous to his colleagues, of all sections and parties, and his *personal* friendship is always valued. Highly sophisticated as a politician, he has, in private, the habit of gracefully waving away mere political differences with an opponent, much as counsel or plaintiff and defendant often go out amicably to lunch together after hurling imprecations at each other through the morning session of court. His hereditary knowledge and acceptance of the necessity and art of political accommodation make him, on most issues, the natural pacificator of the Institution.

He is capable of offering valuable and quite detached purely professional help to a worried colleague, whether Democrat or Republican. He is thoroughly perceptive of the political necessities of the other fellow; but again he will, on *some* subjects, absolutely close his mind to those necessities.

When in 1949 Scott Lucas of Illinois, then the Democratic
Senate leader, was loyally undertaking to carry forward in a
divided Democratic party some of the disputed reforms of
Mr. Truman, his Southern wing was in vehement and un-
ashamed revolt.

With a patience so stolid that eventually it sent him to
hospital with a ruined stomach, he bore week after week
the blows raining upon him not simply from the Republicans
but from his own party brothers to the southward. At length,
unable to bear any more, Lucas one day sadly chided his
Southern colleagues. At once arose Mr. George, the appointed Southern dean, with hoarse and shaking voice, to
repel this outrageous and unprovoked attack. It was
George's view that Lucas had cruelly and without provoca-
tion set upon a great section of *his own party*. The Republicans, even those long in the Institution, sat pop-eyed at
this extraordinary interpretation of the case. Lucas smiled
wryly and spread his wide shoulders.

They liked him, the Southerners, but he was not, after all,
really one of their own, even though there was in his
ancestry some Tennessee "connection."

But when it is Southerners who take up uncharacteristic
and wounding positions—as Lucas was doing, as they saw
it, in attempting to assist a Democratic President—there is
another story entirely. For every such Southern offense save
one there is quick Southern forgiveness. The offender need
not, even momentarily, cease attending the informal Senate

77

caucuses, which are for all the world like the reunions of a large and highly individualistic family whose members are nevertheless bound by the one bond. When he appears after his transgression at these caucuses, the manner is quietly forgiving.

Has cousin William entered upon an unsuitable life by getting, let us say, a little too close to the CIO? Well, this is of course regrettable. But then it is a fact, is it not, that Great Uncle Thomas had a little too much to drink at Vicksburg and had for a time to be removed from command of his battalion?

The one unforgivable sin, the one exception to the policy of easy forgiveness, is to break with the clan upon a point of fundamentals. Senator Estes Kefauver of Tennessee did this, in the Southern Senate view, when early in his career it was represented that he opposed the filibuster. He did it again when, in his "Crime Investigation" in 1951 and 1952 he seemed to the Southerners to be undertaking to tell the States and municipalities what to do about their crime problems—and to be bathing in questionable publicity.

For a time, by means as airy as a cloud but as cold as sleet, he was informally banished from the political company of the Senate Southerners generally. This fact was one of the least-known and most important circumstances of the 1952 Democratic Presidential convention.

Kefauver went there with impressive evidence of the public support for the Democratic Presidential nomination.

He never approached that nomination, in fact, and would not have, had the convention run three solid months instead of a week. The Southerners, though not in position affirmatively to direct the convention, nevertheless had, with powerful allies from the North, quite enough power to block Kefauver. No other Southern purpose was so fixed, so implacable. The Southerners, moreover, in 1956 fought his nomination for Vice-President as long as they could stand and fight.

The only other Southern Senator I ever knew to break with the clan totally was Claude Pepper of Florida. The sense of Southern alienation from this able, indeed this brilliant, man, was more subtle. It lay in a belief, justified or not, that Pepper was fundamentally *un-Southern*, perhaps in part because for a time his views on foreign policy seemed clearly those of the very advanced left wing, however he intended them to look.

In any case, there was a Southern wall against Pepper in the Senate. It was so hostile a wall that the ordinarily tolerant and imperturbable Byrd once, without the slightest rebuke from the chair, declared of Senator Pepper from the Senate floor that he had learned never to dispute with "a skunk."

VII

THE SENATE

AND THE CLUB

WHEN one unexpectedly needs a room in a good, and crowded, hotel in New York like the Pierre, which is not so very long on tradition, his best course is to approach the clerk in masterful determination, allowing no other assumption at all than that he will be accommodated. When such a need rises in a traditional hotel abroad, say Brown's in London, the wiser attitude is precisely the reverse. There it is better to approach the subject wearily and a bit hopelessly and to say to the clerk, of course I know it is hardly possible that you could find a place for me.

When one enters the House of Representatives, or becomes an official in the Executive Department, the sound attitude is not simply to put the best foot forward, but to stamp it for emphasis—in front of the photographers if any are present, and if official superiors are not. But when one enters the Senate he comes into a different place altogether. The long custom of the place impels him, if he is at all wise, to walk with a soft foot and to speak with a soft voice, and infrequently. Men who have reached national fame in less than two years in powerful non-Senatorial office—Saltonstall as Governor of Massachusetts, Duff as Governor of Pennsylvania for recent examples—have found four years and more not to be long enough to feel free to speak up loudly in the Institution. All the newcomer needs, if he is able and strong, is the passage of time—but this he needs indispensably, save in those rare cases where the authentic geniuses among Senate types are involved.

The old definition of the Senate as "the most exclusive club in the world" is no longer altogether applicable, as perhaps it never was. It *is*, however, both a club and a club within a club. By the newly arrived and by some of the others the privileges are only carefully and sparingly used. To the senior members—and sometimes they are senior only in terms of power and high acceptability—privilege is inexhaustible and can be pressed to almost any limit. I have seen one member, say a Lehman of New York, confined by niggling and almost brutal Senate action to the most literal inhibitions of the least important of all the rules. And again I have seen a vital Senate roll call held off by all sorts of openly dawdling time-killing for hours, in spite of the fact that supposedly it is not possible to interrupt a roll call once it is in motion, for the simple purpose of seeing that a delayed aircraft has opportunity to land at Washington Airport so that a motorcycle escort can bring, say a Humphrey of Minnesota in to be recorded.

Lehman was, of course, a member of the Outer Club, which is composed of all the Senate. But Humphrey is, in part by the mysterious operation of acceptability-by-association, in or very close to the Inner Club. The inequality indicated here has nothing to do with political belief or activity; both Lehman and Humphrey are liberal Democrats and both have records of distinction. Humphrey simply got along better.

The inner life of the Senate—and the vast importance to it of its internal affairs may be seen in the fact that it has on occasion taken longer to decide upon the proper salaries for a handful of Senate employees than to provide billions of dollars for the defense of the United States—is controlled by

83

the Inner Club. This is an organism without name or charter, without officers, without a list of membership, without a wholly conscious being at all.

There is no list of qualifications for membership, either posted or orally mentioned. At the core of the Inner Club stand the Southerners, who with rare exceptions automatically assume membership almost with the taking of the oath of office. They get in, so to speak, by inheritance, but at their elbows within the core are others, Easterners, Midwesterners, Westerners, Republicans or Democrats.

The outer life of the Senate, in which all the members are theoretically more or less equal at the time of decision that comes when a roll-call vote is added up, is defined by its measurable actions on bills and on public policies. But this outer life, even in its most objective aspects, is not free of the subtle influence of the inner life of the Institution.

The inner life is in the command of a distinct minority within this place of the minority. This minority-within-a-minority is the Inner Club. This Inner Club, though in spirit largely dominated by the Southerners, is by no means geographic.

Those who belong to it express, consciously or unconsciously, the deepest instincts and prejudices of "the Senate type." The Senate type is, speaking broadly, a man for whom the Institution is a career in itself, a life in itself and an end in itself. This Senate type is not always free of Presidential ambition, a striking case in point having been the late Senator

Taft. But the important fact is that when the Senate type thinks of the Presidency he thinks of it as only *another* and not as really a *higher* ambition, as did Taft and as did Senator Russell of Georgia when, in 1952, he sought the Democratic Presidential nomination.

The Senate type makes the Institution his home in an almost literal sense, and certainly in a deeply emotional sense. His head swims with its history, its lore and the accounts of past personnel and deeds and purposes. To him, precedent has an almost mystical meaning and where the common run of members will reflect twice at least before creating a precedent, the Senate type will reflect so long and so often that nine times out of ten he will have nothing to do with such a project at all.

His concern for the preservation of Senate tradition is so great that he distrusts anything out of the ordinary, however small, as for example a night session. Not necessarily an abstemious man (and sometimes a fairly bibulous one as a convivial character *within* the Institution) he will complain that such sessions, especially along toward the closing days of Congress, will be unduly tiring on the elders of the body. Often he really means here that prolonged meetings, tending as they do to send the most decorous of men out to the lounges for a nip, may wind up with one or more distinguished members taking aboard what never in the world would be called a few too many.

This Senate type knows, with the surest touch in the world,

85

precisely how to treat his colleagues, Outer Club as well as Inner Club. He is nearly always a truly compassionate man, very slow to condemn his brothers. And not even the imminent approach of a great war can disturb him more than the approach of what he may regard as adequate evidence that the Senate may in one crisis or another be losing not the affection of the country (for which he has no great care) but the *respect* of the country.

He measures the degree of respect being shown by the country at any given time not wholly by what he reads and hears through the mass media, and not at all by the indicated attitude of any President, but by what is borne in upon his consciousness by his contact with what he considers to be the more *suitable* conveyors of *proper* public thought. He, the true Senate type, has this partiality toward the few as distinguished from the many all through his career even though he will hide it skillfully in his recurring tests at home when, up for re-election, he *must* depend upon the mass.

As the Southern members of the Inner Club make the ultimate decisions as to what is proper in point of manner— these decisions then infallibly pervading the Outer Club— so the whole generality of the Inner Club makes the decisions as to what *in general* is proper in the Institution and what *in general* its conclusions should be on high issues. These decisions are in no way overtly or formally reached; it is simply that one day the perceptive onlooker will discover a kind of aura from the Inner Club that informs him of what the Senate is later going to do about such and such.

For an illustration of the point, there was this small but significant incident in 1956: Some of the junior members had set out to put some Congressional check on the Central Intelligence Agency by creating an overseeing Joint Congressional Committee. A majority of the whole body became formally committed to the bill, and all seemed clear ahead. Suddenly, however, some of the patriarchs—among them the venerable Alben Barkley of Kentucky, who was soon to die in his seventy-ninth year while smiting the Republicans from a speaking platform at Washington and Lee University —found themselves disenchanted. They decided, for no very perceptible reason except that they felt they had been inadequately consulted, that a joint committee would not do at all. Under their bleak and languid frowns the whole project simply died; a wind had blown upon it from the Inner Club and its erstwhile sponsors simply left it.

The Senate type therefore—and his distillate as found in the Inner Club—is in many senses more an institutional man than a public man in the ordinary definition of such a personage. Some of the Senate's most powerful public men have not been truly Senate types. The late Senator Arthur Vandenberg of Michigan, for all his influence upon foreign relations after he had abandoned isolationism for internationalism, was never in his career a true Senate type, no matter how formidable he was as a public man. Incomparably the truest current Senate type, and incomparably the most influential man on the inner life of the Senate, Senator Russell of Georgia, has never had one-tenth Vandenberg's impact upon public and press in objective, or out-Senate, affairs.

Russell's less palpable and less measurable influence, however, was infinitely greater in the *Senate*, on all matters involving its inner being, than was Vandenberg's, as indeed was Taft's. For Russell could actually command the votes of others upon many matters, even some entirely objective matters. Vandenberg spoke to the country and occasionally to the world. Russell (and the other Senate types as well) speaks primarily to the Senate. Going back a good deal farther, Huey Long of Louisiana spoke also beyond the Senate, specifically to the discontented and the dispossessed outside, while one of his greatest critics of the time, Carter Glass of Virginia, spoke to the Senate, as Byrd of Virginia does to this day.

The non-Senate types, it thus may be seen, are in the end influential only to the degree that they may so instruct or so inflame a part of the public sufficiently large to insist upon this or that course of political conduct. The Senate type in the last analysis has the better of it. For not only does his forum generally resist change and all public pressure save the massive and enduring; it also will tend quickly to adopt *his* proposals unless they are quite clearly untenable.

The Senate Democratic leader in the Eighty-fourth Congress, Lyndon Johnson of Texas, once was able to pass more than a hundred bills, not all of them lacking in controversy, in a matter of a little more than an hour. There were a variety or reasons for this wholly untypical burst of speed in a body devoted to the leisurely approach. But the most important of these reasons was simply "Lyndon wants it." It is hardly necessary to add that "Lyndon" is pre-eminently a Senate type, so much so that, highly realistic politician though he is, he is quite unable to believe that the public is not in utter fascination of the parliamentary procedures of his Institution.

Again the Republican Senate leader, Knowland of California (and like Johnson he is senior only in terms of place and power and not in years) is a curious example of the power of the Senate type. Knowland, who inherited the leadership in a personal laying on of hands from the dying Senator Taft, was in both the Eighty-third and Eighty-fourth Congresses in what one might have thought to be a position scarcely likely to win him great popularity in his party or in the Senate.

A young Republican of the old school, he was faithful in his fashion to the newly arrived Republican in the White House, General Eisenhower, but he persisted, it will be recalled, in rebellious notions about Asian policy and about dealing with the world Communists. There were many times when, in the Senate and before the world, he was clearly contradicting an almost ecstatically popular Republican President of the United States and all the powerful forces in that President's train.

Outsiders could not quite see how Knowland could in these

circumstances remain the President's party spokesman in the Senate. The Senate types, for their part, simply could not grasp what the outsiders were talking about. To the Inner Club it was sheer nonsense to talk of Knowland as the *President's* leader; plainly he was the *Senate's* leader, on one side of the aisle.

There arose some talk among the "Eisenhower Republicans" of trying to displace Knowland as leader. It died, embarrassedly, in the throats of its utterers before the stern reproof of the Senate type—in both parties, if it comes to that.

A man, therefore, may be a Senate type in good standing in the Inner Club if he is wholly out of step on fateful matters with his own Administration (as with Knowland on Asia in regard to Eisenhower). He may be the same if he is wholly out of step with his own party, as for illustration Byrd in regard to the regular Democrats who control the party nationally. He may be the same if, like McClellan of Arkansas he comes fortuitously and reluctantly to national attention only because he becomes involved in something widely televised, like the Army-McCarthy hearings.

Equally a man may be a powerful Senate type with never a great legislative triumph to his credit, by a mysterious chemical process that seems to be transforming now so relative a newcomer as Payne of Maine. Why such progress for Payne? It is a little awkward to explain; perhaps the explanation is that Payne, who was a rather hard-handed politician as Governor of Maine, simply generates a warmth about him because he so wholeheartedly performs, without fuss or trouble, such Senate chores as are handed over to him.

The converse is similarly so. William Fulbright of Arkansas, a Rhodes Scholar, an ex-university president, a young and literate man with many useful years ahead of him, was credited as a member of the House with promoting this country's turn to internationalism before the Second World War. He has been credited since in the Senate with many achievements, not the least of which is the cumulative achievement of an experience and a seniority that are very likely one day to make him chairman of the Foreign Relations Committee.

He is not, for all of this, quite a Senate type. Nor, for another example, is Paul Douglas of Illinois, with his academic background, his ability in the field of economics, and his not inconsiderable feat in winning re-election in 1954 over assistance given to his opponent by President Eisenhower. Is scholastic achievement or "intellectualism" then—considering the cases of Fulbright and of Douglas—some bar to the Inner Club? Not at all. For, standing well inside the doors of the Inner Club, at least, is Humphrey of Minnesota, who used to teach political science. And at the very heart of the Inner Club in the Eighty-fourth Congress sat the man with what many would consider the most truly intellectual character in the Senate, Eugene Millikin of Colorado.

Does being liberal put a barrier on the way to the Inner

Club? No, for few in the Institution can be more liberal than the old indestructible, Senator Theodore Green of Rhode Island, a member of the very hierarchy of the Club.

Does being "unpopular" and remote keep out a man? No. The ordinary conversation of Carl Hayden of Arizona, whose manners are as leathery as his face, consists largely of sour grunts. And Hayden could very nearly be the president of the Club, if only it had officers.

Does wealth or social status count? Not really. One of those men in the Senate who are wholly without commercial instinct and must get along strictly on their salaries is Mike Mansfield of Montana. He spent his young years in the mines of Butte; he largely educated himself—and he, like Humphrey, is well across the threshold of the Inner Club. And, unlike Humphrey, Mansfield has no gift at all for gregariousness; at Senatorial parties one sees him standing aloof, his eyes and voice quiet, smoking his pipe and leaving as soon as departure is at all possible. Knowland, too, is less than a relaxed social being. Earnest, conscientious and loyal though he is, he is almost without a sense of humor—but not without a sense of tolerance.

Indeed, it may be that this is one of the keys to the qualities of the Senate type—tolerance toward his fellows, intolerance toward any who would in any real way change the Senate, its customs or its way of life. And, right or wrong, it is the moral force of these men that gives to them an ascendancy in the Institution which they never assert and which most of them do nothing consciously to promote.

It is, then, against all this background of the human facts in the case that answer must be made to the question whether and how the Senate is "the most exclusive club in the world" and whether, indeed it is exclusive in the ordinary understanding at all.

Certainly there is in the common definition nothing exclusive in a place in which a Taft, with his almost religious feeling about party orthodoxy, for years sat so amicably and by choice beside an Aiken of Vermont, whose Republicanism had, by Taft's standards, some sadly thin spots in its fabric. Where the son of an Alabama sharecropper, Sparkman of Alabama, has shared so many projects in social legislation with the rich, aloof Murray of Montana. Where the son of Huey Long, Senator Russell Long of Louisiana, so atypically carries on the dynasty by habitual quietude and responsibility in the seat that his father made so clangorous and so irresponsible. Where a Prescott Bush of Connecticut, late of St. George's School, Newport, R. I., and still later of Brown Brothers Harriman & Co. of Wall Street, has shared a forum with a Pastore of Rhode Island, late of the public schools of the city of Providence and of Northeastern University.

There *is*, however, for all of this, a quality of exclusiveness, too. Though some arrive more or less by accident in the Senate, most have worked a passage that has required more than luck, than money, than family or political position. In a sense at first there is the exclusiveness of success and then, as test succeeds test, the exclusiveness of both success and understanding. All these may be, and are, attained without reaching the final quality of exclusiveness that is involved in acceptance in the Inner Club.

To be in the Inner Club a man must be many things—some important and some mere accidents of life—but the greatest of these things is to have the character that will pass the severest scrutiny (if carried out blandly and seemingly casually) of which nearly five score highly understanding and humanly perceptive men are capable.

It is not character in the sense intended in the forms prepared by personnel offices. It has not got much to do with questions like "Does applicant drink?" or "Does he pay his bills?" It is character in the sense that only the true traditionalists will understand.

It is character in the sense that the special integrity of the person must be in harmony with, and not lesser in its way than, the special integrity of the Institution—the integrity of its oneness.

VIII

THE SENATE

AND THE LEADERSHIPS

THE SENATE always has had two duly chosen leaders, one for the majority and one for the minority. But the questions as to how and when (and sometimes whether) they really lead are open to a variety of answers. In this business there is no constant. The ways of the place are passing strange and the personalities and purposes of the various leaders are highly individual and highly at variance. There is in fact not even any fixed and general concept of just what a leader is and just what he *ought* to do, except that when the Senate is in characteristic mood and tone there is general agreement on what he is *not* and what he ought *not* to do.

In all but those rare and comparatively brief periods when it is thrust into the background by extraordinary circumstances, such as the imperatives of a great war or the transient dominance over the whole political structure of a Franklin Roosevelt, the Senate expects of its leaders:

That he who is a member of the party holding the White House will not so much represent the President as the Senate itself.

That he who is a member of the party that lost the Presidency will represent not so much that party as the Senate itself.

That each will consider himself primarily the spokesman for a group in the *Senate* and not so much for any group in the country or any non-Senatorial political organism whatever, not excluding the Republican and Democratic National Committee organizations.

In abnormal times (and the Senate though capable of behaving well in crisis is alien to all crisis action and dreads the mere thought of it) all this view of what is properly to

96

be expected of a floor leader will be perforce altered. It will be altered simply by the unfeeling hand of overpowering circumstance much as the ordinary life of a young man is turned quite about at the moment the mail brings him that well-known communication from the draft board in which are extended to him certain greetings from the President of the United States.

On such occasions the Institution concedes what it cannot sensibly deny—that is, that for the time being the leaders must cast their glances outward and cease being absolutely Senatorial. Though endlessly yearning for a return of the old day, as the young man undergoing basic Army training in the swamps of Louisiana yearns for the ultimate discharge, the Senate leader, too, must in the meantime make his sacrifices and allow his whole manner of doing things to be wrenched out of shape.

Just as the Senate during the War Between the States in part suspended the historic guarantees of unlimited debate and even agreed during the First World War to tinker with its rules, so in other times of passion and peril it will allow *momentary* revision of the functions of its leaders. There was such a time when Mr. Roosevelt in his urgent haste to save the economic life of the nation was causing in the House the passing of bills of which the only immediately available simulations were rolled-up newspapers.

The Institution, it goes without saying, never went nearly so far as this, not even in an era in which Congress generally

97

was perhaps at its lowest point of power and the Executive at its highest. Nevertheless, in the first such clear instance in history, there arose a highly oversimplified public notion of the duties of Senate leadership based on the assumption that a leader of Democrats in the Senate *necessarily* owed obedience to a Democratic President. The compulsive actions of the Senate itself, which even at that hour intellectually rebelled in the deepest sense, for a time had the effect of promoting what the Senate felt to be a profound heresy.

For however pragmatically useful such an arrangement may be said to be, it is in fact demonstrably heretical unless one wishes to overturn the triune system of government that is fundamental to all. But, heresy or not, the notion has shown uncommon virility among the public, as witness the late Congress in which men very high in the Eisenhower Administration honestly felt that Senator Knowland of California simply had no *right* as the Republican leader to denounce Administration policy on China.

The Senate itself has been wholly unimpressed; doggedly it has remained engaged upon the task to which it had dedicated itself for some years. This purpose was, as far as possible, to expunge from its history what its principal members felt to have been the regrettable abasement of the Institution in the Roosevelt time.

Knowland, therefore, far from overextending his credit in the Institution as Republican leader, became in a way ever more acceptable to it during the Eisenhower years. This was not because his China views were thought to be *right* but rather because there had appeared upon sensitive Senate antennae the faint preliminary shocks which it was feared just *might* signal another gathering attack from a powerful White House on the privilege of this or any Senate leader. To strike at those privileges is, in a true sense, to strike at the privileges of the Institution itself; no man there is an island to himself.

Nearly the whole of the Truman Administration, the first two years of the Eisenhower Administration and then, in the Eighty-fourth Congress, in the latter half of that Administration—through all this span of time the Senate was recovering the ground of prestige that had been for a time ceded before overwhelming force in the Roosevelt era.

Thus, the Eighty-fourth Congress may fairly be described as affording, ideally, a typical field for examining the operations of Senate leadership, as an instrument, in its traditional cast. This is not to say that the *personnel* of this leadership, Knowland for the Republicans and Johnson for the Democrats, was itself typical or average. That is another tale altogether and will later be told.

In the institutional sense, however, the marshalship of both parties was in the hands of men holding the classic view of their rights and powers, however they differed, from each other and from their prototypes of the past, as to how to implement these rights and powers.

Knowland, as was true of Taft before him, never for a

99

moment forgot the *basic* Senate conviction that he was the Republican leader of the *Senate*. He sought, as far as he could, to promote there such policies of the President as he could in good conscience endorse or accept; but he let it go at this point. In dealing with what is traditionally a more disciplined party than the Democratic party confronting him across the aisle, the tactics of his leadership were, as is so often the case among the Republicans, both reserved and lacking in open urgency.

It was his habit to assume a fundamental Republican unity, and since he stood at the head of a comparatively untemperamental group of Senate Republicans he undertook none of the subtleties that are necessary in dealing with real prima donnas, just as he rarely attempted anything in the way of issuing party ukases or commands upon the rank and file.

In unspoken accord with Johnson across the aisle, Knowland in short took no step that did not on balance promote the claims of the Senate against those of the White House. In this indispensable respect the two, though one had his party's chief in the White House, formed models of the perfect leadership as the Institution sees it.

But while it was Knowland who was pictured across the country as the great rebel against constituted authority, the greater rebel and the even more thorough Senate man, in fact, was Johnson.

For where Knowland from the Republican side was proclaiming the Senate's substantial separateness from the current Republican White House, Johnson was quietly moving from the Democratic side to proclaim its *independence* from *any* White House and, indeed, its independence to a point from his own party.

His real purpose was at the start only tactical, to strengthen the political center by a series of accommodations first within the Democratic rank and file and then between this now consolidated Democratic rank and file and the Republican rank and file. The *effect* of what he did, however, was something else again. It amounted to a very long extension, even by Senate standards, of the historic claim of the place to an independent political life within the theoretically merged trinity of Constitutional powers—Executive, Legislative and Judicial.

Taft, the great Republican, in the last months of his life, using the stuff of Senate tradition as the most important of his raw materials and adding to this some typically Taftian notions, had set out to make an extraordinary rationale of his place in the scheme of things. Rejecting without a moment's hesitation any notion that *he,* as a Senator's Senator, should *represent* the Republican President, General Eisenhower, Taft hit upon the plan that in certain very important matters *he* would actually *lead* the President.

Johnson, then newly arrived to leadership on his side of the chamber, watched with the most sympathetic perception this Taftian policy, which had, of course enormous attraction to any true Senate type. When fortune put the Democrats in

101

control of the Senate in 1955, the Texan pupil was prepared to adapt and then to outdo the evolution that the Ohio mentor had so lately brought about.

All this Johnson approached with scrupulous caution. He was not only a young man, then only forty-six years old, but he had served only six years in the Institution, which is on the whole inclined to regard such a span of time as no more than a mere beginning. He was at the head, primarily through the benevolent though admiring patronage of the powerful chief of the Southern clan, Senator Russell, of a party that was in great difficulties. The party and even its membership in the Senate (for this ultimate fact of general political life not even they could escape) had suffered deep divisions from about midway in the second term of Franklin Roosevelt. And these divisions had been rubbed up in the Truman years.

Johnson, moreover, was himself, of course, a Southerner. But while at the last moment he would always be one, he had the greatest necessity to make not merely a peace but a genuine comity of association with the non-Southerners among the other Senate Democrats. These demanded of him more than merely Southern attitudes, though the Southerners were quietly conscious that in the end they had first claim upon him. Finally, he had the ever-present human problem that would confront any young man called suddenly to lead men so much his elders in years, in service and (so they thought at first) in truly experienced appreciation of the Institution.

102

Faced with all this complex of affairs, and knowing that one major false step would destroy him as a leader, Johnson had to find a way to bring together the Democratic right (George, Byrd and company) and the Democratic left (Humphrey, Lehman and company) and to do this in such a way as not intolerably to endanger the vital interests or fundamental convictions of either.

Here was a problem, indeed, in the proper exercise of the Calhoun Doctrine of the Concurrent Majority!

Manifestly, the first necessity was to find *some* areas upon which all could agree, and these areas when found, were necessarily somewhat thin, sometimes rather dusty with age, and always deeply traditional. (For example, it was not hard to lead the whole Democratic side of the Senate to adopt and restate the ancient general Democratic accusation that the Republicans were the party of "the rich." To all the Democrats this was accepted doctrine.)

But the more success crowned these efforts at safely bringing together the Democrats *within the Senate*, the more disappointed and perturbed became the non-Senatorial Democrats generally and particularly the normal partisan Democratic instruments such as the National Committee. The National Committee was not enchanted. Nor were the aspirants for the 1956 Presidential nomination. Where, in this state of affairs, was a truly broad complex of issues to be made?

The non-Senatorial Democrats began to make complaint that Democratic unity in the Senate was all very well; but

103

what of the millions of non-Senatorial Democrats as against the few in the Institution? What of the national, the state, the county and city and ward organizations? What sort of record was being made in the Senate for these sinews, these repositories of the blood and guts, of the party? Who could win a campaign in '56 on co-operation?

Johnson for his part, now driven by unfolding events perhaps farther than he would have chosen had he had his way, retorted, in the grand Senatorial manner, that the Senate would make high policy as it saw fit. The party organisms would kindly confine their work to what the Senate saw as their traditionally proper sphere—that is, to routine digging, research, money raising, arrangements for television broadcasts and the like.

It fell out, therefore, that 1955 and 1956 saw a great and progressive philosophic alienation between the Democrats of the Senate and, in a sense, the Democrats of the United States, especially those of the North. Johnson now began developing a philosophy by which the Democratic leader of the Senate was responsible *only* and not merely primarily to the Institution. He had no hesitation in asserting that it was no part of his responsibility to prepare material, in the form of issues or otherwise, for a national Presidential campaign. It was his job to guide the Senate.

From all this, of course, there arose a cloud of intriguing implications; for present purposes the relevant point is this: Knowland and Johnson, true Senate types, had between them struck an informal bargain to protect and defend the true faith. But Johnson, fortuitously or not and unintentionally or not, had also done a great deal more. He had not merely preserved the Senate's view of the proper leadership; he had immeasurably extended the doctrine that the leadership, and above and beyond that the Institution, was *an end in itself.*

Though the meaning of what he and Knowland did was of a pattern, their separate *means* were different. Where Knowland as leader largely took up the aloof posture of the commanding general back at headquarters, leaving the details of field leadership to subordinates, Johnson went down to the very platoons.

Endlessly he was at it, cajoling, entreating, flattering, blandly threatening, sometimes saying words and taking actions that would have been forgiven in none other than a Senate type. The elders in his party he sought to spare the hard spade work; he would call upon them to rise in debate only in the last resort of extreme crisis. The younger men he drove and lashed, as he drove and lashed even the ordinarily faceless Senate staff and committee employees.

But where Johnson risked all for the sake of intraparty accommodation, Taft before him had been a great Senate leader precisely *because* his whole spirit was alien and hostile to party accommodation. Taft, in a small chamber where men are close, had been a great leader *because* he was, in a way, always pointedly alone. Going a bit further back, Alben Barkley of Kentucky, later to become Mr. Truman's Vice-

President and still later to be returned to the Senate, had been a *good* leader *because* he was convivial, garrulous, cheerfully ready to take his lumps from day to day. Scott Lucas of Illinois had been a *good* leader because, like Johnson of Texas later, he believed in party accommodation—but not a great leader, because the weapons of accommodation did not neatly function in his hands. But Barkley, also a good leader, was untypical in this matter of accommodation; it was his habit to press on without compromise to the end.

And Ernest McFarland of Arizona had been only a fair leader, if that, because of what can only be called an unconquerable and overweening tolerance. There are not many times when a Senate leader can afford to "get tough"; to McFarland there was no time at all. The late Kenneth Wherry of Nebraska had been a fair to good leader—but his outstanding characteristic in the post was a flatly uncompromising attitude and a brand of Midwestern, small-town, Lions Club Republicanism so intolerant as sometimes to repel even the redoubtable Taft.

In this, as in so many other things, nothing goes by rule of thumb in the Senate. Distinction is the commonplace; the average does not really exist.

IX

THE MAKING

OF A SENATOR

THE MAKING of a good Senator is in some ways similar to the making of a work of art. There are few short cuts; the longest way round is the surest way home. The career must usually

107

rest upon what is slowly developing and enduring, if not necessarily what is popularly "right" at a given time, rather than what is quick and spectacular. It must, moreover, be based upon a field of action that is inherently suitable to the Institution over the long common slope of its being. The air of reflectiveness is the breath of life in this place. Eminence may be reached by a concentration on frenetic and untypical Senatorial activity but it will never be sustained in that way. In the period roughly from 1950 to 1955 a handful of Senate "red hunters," most of them quite junior in the place and hardly any of them influential in its inner workings, were incomparably more publicized than the eighty-odd others not so engaged. McCarthy . . . Jenner . . . Eastland . . . McCarran . . . These and a few others, busy with accusation rather than with law-making and policy-making and debate, were the headline names. But the period was an aberration and before 1955 was out not even the Great Investigator, McCarthy himself, could compete for attention, outside or inside the Senate, with its traditional men.

For the good Senator is the product, and necessarily so considering the character of the place itself, of what has general and fundamental meaning in political life. Daniel Webster of New Hampshire is one of the great Senate men of history, in spite of his frank dedication to the vested interests of his State, because of his preoccupation above all with a subject of properly Senatorial stature, the unthinkability of secession and the preservation of the Union. It was not that his course always was popular or even necessarily correct; at times his view angered much of the North as altogether too broad-minded while it enraged the South as intolerably close-minded. It was simply that his issue was big enough and grand enough for the forum in which he sat.

Webster in short was concerned with a great and lasting question, the proper relationship of the States to the Federal power. Taft of Ohio was a great Senator for similar reasons. For all his shortcomings (the majestic wrongheadedness that was perhaps as damaging in its way as was Webster's pompous vanity and self-indulgence) Taft too was a man not of an hour or of a day but of a space in history. *His* concern was with nothing less than the relationship of the individual to the Federal power—in the fields of labor, finance, civil rights, housing, health and nearly all the rest. Whether his conclusions were correct did not so much concern the Senate as that they so fittingly ranged over such wide areas of life. His inconsistencies, particularly in matters of foreign affairs, were, whatever else they may have been, *large* inconsistencies.

The late Vandenberg of Michigan was a good Senator because of his historic role in changing the minds of a large section of his respectable Republican following to the point where it would willingly contemplate a deliverance of the party to an internationalism it had theretofore greatly distrusted.

And not only were these exemplars occupied with general

109

and lasting subjects; they also were intently and consecutively and tirelessly so occupied. None of them attempted the dispersion of effort that has handicapped and even ruined many Senatorial careers; each knew precisely where he was going. Equally important, each knew the limit to which by old and unspoken Senate custom he could press his designs; the limits of tolerance.

But when a much more recent Senator, Humphrey of Minnesota, came to the Institution he had already far overrun that line of the tolerable. He nevertheless became a good Senator because of what happened afterward. As a reform Mayor of Minneapolis he had become the hero of a liberal movement indigenous to the upper Middle West and as a delegate to the 1948 Democratic National Convention in Philadelphia he was shortly to become one of the heroes of the liberal movement nationally.

At that convention, the Democratic party appeared even to its oldest and most loyal partisan leaders to be in very poor shape for the Presidential contest shortly to come.

It had, two years before, lost Congress to the Republicans for the first time in half a generation and less recently it had lost its greatest modern leader, Franklin Roosevelt. The then President, Mr. Truman, had not by that time been recognized for the major contributions to history that he had made, as he is not now fully recognized for these and the other contributions that later he made. No political estimate was more general than the estimate that the

110

Democrats were very likely to lose the 1948 elections and that such a loss would become a moral certainty if the convention further inflamed a Democratic South-North division over civil rights.

All was accordingly arranged among the party leaders, in both factions, to deal softly in the platform with this highly sensitive issue. The platform committee duly brought out a carefully diluted document. Humphrey, a member of the committee and then only an aspirant to the Senate, would have none of this. He took to the convention floor, where it could not and did not lose, an appeal for a civil rights plank far more acceptable to the North than to the South.

Many will recall what followed: the angry march out into the rain of some of the Deep Southern delegations, the enfevered scene on the convention floor which even the most faithful considered a sure prelude to Democratic disaster in the following November. It did not, to be sure, turn out that way: Mr. Truman won after all and the Democrats regained Congress.

The point now, however, was that Humphrey, even before reaching the Institution in that November, and long before transgressing the amenities in his attack on Byrd's Joint Committee, had broken the most underlying of all the unwritten rules. He had rejected the greatest political *raison d'être* of the Institution, the function of political compromise, and in the process he had made rude gestures toward those who were shortly to be his powerful Senatorial elders.

111

The road lay lonely and hostile before him, in consequence, when he appeared in the Senate to take the oath of
office. The Outer Club was open to him only in the sense
that all who belong to the Institution must belong to it. The
Inner Club, at this point, lay immeasurably beyond any
reckoning of hope for him.

What then, in the pursuit of this particular case history
in the making of a Senator, saved Humphrey—or, more
specifically, what was it that from this beginning made him
a good Senator after all? Primarily there was the fact that
though he had beyond doubt outraged the essential Doctrine
of the Concurrent Majority these things, at least, *could* be
said of him: His intolerable activities at Philadelphia had
in any case occurred before he had been schooled in the
Institution. Thus it could be urged in his behalf, by those
who wished to give him a chance, that his had been an
unconscious rather than a willful heresy. And it had to be admitted that his issue, however painfully he had insisted upon
drawing it, was not a merely trifling or truly un-Senatorial
one. (The Senate's instinctive memory could not wholly
dismiss the fact that something akin to young Mr. Humphrey's issue in fact had been quite prominent in its affairs
in another century, in the time of Webster and Calhoun.)

Finally, to a body of old men Humphrey was quite young
and there was a certain tendency to forgive error in the
young.

More important than all these considerations, however, his

slow ascent to grace was the clear, but far from simple, fact that he had in him so many *latently* Senatorial qualities.

Not long had he been around before it became evident that, notwithstanding his regrettable past, he had a tactile sense of the moods and the habits and the mind of the place. Where another newcomer of the class of '48, Kefauver of Tennessee, seemed somehow usually to do the wrong thing at the right time, Humphrey seemed progressively to do things right. Where, for example, Kefauver suffered from a sad-eyed ebullience of highly personal effort that however worthy was notably disparate—from investigating crime to supporting some unlikely project like Atlantic Union— Humphrey unerringly set his purposes to be in harmony with the forms and spirit of the place.

He did not at all abandon his liberal designs (though as to civil rights the unyielding facts of life in the Senate forced him to move upon a zigzag course). He largely confined himself, however, to such suitably traditional liberal issues as higher farm subsidies and more generous labor laws. But he pursued these in complete awareness that in this body the best of motives will languish away unless one is able to marshal for them at best the support and at worst the fairly benevolent neutrality of at least some of the true Senate types.

Having recognized the nature of the problem Humphrey went about finding the human means with which to meet it. Unhurriedly—easy does it—and more or less naturally

113

he fell into the habit of forgathering with the Democratic leader, Senator Johnson of Texas, and through Johnson there shortly developed a line of communication, however strained at first, with the other Southerners. With these Humphrey kept up a running and good-humored private debate, in the Senate lounges and on private occasions.

As he came really to know them, and particularly the able Senatorial politician who is Johnson, he began to suspect that there was, even on such matters as civil rights, less of blood-in-the-nostrils to their approach than he had supposed. And they came to suspect the same thing about him.

Slowly, by this means, Humphrey began to be taken into the informal and decisive deliberations of the Democratic hierarchs, if only as a spokesman among these centrists of a liberal view that did not characterize either his party there or the Institution itself. To be brought in one way or another into this sort of deliberation is indispensable to becoming a good Senator, for such recognition foreshadows recognition for assignment to the committees from which one draws the greater part of his power in the Senate.

It is, however, a recognition that does not and will not come to those who fail to seek it or, seeking it, lack the peculiarly perceptive touch first to solicit perquisite without seeming to hunger for it and second to exercise perquisite without seeming to abuse it. (Abuse of perquisite is left to the long-established in the Senate; and in their case it is deemed no longer abuse but only the free exercise of what are regarded as the inherent and inalienable powers of the seniors in the Inner Club.)

Indeed, Humphrey had found, and now he illustrated, one of the ultimate truths of the Senate. This is that one *cannot* forever refuse there to make any compromise at all and remain a good, or effective, member. The art of high negotiation is an absolutely necessary part of Senatorial equipment. For the Institution, as it was at its beginning, is something more than a parliamentary body engaged upon parliamentary work. It is likewise an assemblage of diplomatists, in which each State in a sense sends Ambassadors to the Federal Republic, and the function of Ambassadors is not to reach proud, violent disagreement; it is, of course, to find acceptable agreement.

To accomplish this and yet not to let down one's principles, one's side, one's State—this is the unique achievement of a good Senate man. Because this is the highest requisite, it follows that this is no place for the man who has *only* principle; for every genuine political fanatic is simply awash with principle as he understands the term.

Humphrey, in short, as will all others new to the Senate, had found, and quite honestly found, that the career he had prefaced by scorning at the Philadelphia Convention the concept of necessary compromise would proceed in the Senate only to the degree that he accepted the inevitability, and even the desirability, of just that concept. The vehement heretic of yesterday had now embraced, perforce and indeed happily as his understanding grew, the Doctrine According to the Senate.

The tolerance of dissent—to a degree practiced in no other parliamentary body—that is characteristic of the place had now enabled Humphrey to find his home. In the process there had been a mutual erosion of views—his earlier views had to some extent been altered by the conservative views at which he had chipped. And those views had been somewhat altered by his.

By the year 1956 this circumstance had been interpreted by some of his more advanced liberal friends as a surrender to "reaction." And these, who had exulted when he took the lead on civil rights at Philadelphia, now began to fall away from him. It cannot readily be denied, however, that the more moderate Humphrey of the late fifties had, in consequence of all that had happened to him, put himself in infinitely better position to bring the Senate to adopt *some* bill in that area.

Because he was no longer looked at doubtfully by the Senate types (for an important illustration of this point) he was able in the Eighty-fourth Congress to bring off, by a *unanimous* Senate vote, one of the most cherished objectives alike of the liberals and of the true conservatives. This was the establishment, over the initial opposition of the Eisenhower Administration itself, of an independent commission to review the operations of the Government's loyalty-security program. A man not so acceptable simply could not conceivably have done this, however fine might have been his bill.

Thus, the making of a good Senator involves several intangibles: A credible emanation of ultimate good faith in what he is about, one of the main criteria of good faith being the absence of petty exhibitionism. An understanding acceptance of the requirement of compromise, and therefore a willingness to abide dissent. A concentration upon the coherent and important and an avoidance of the diffuse and doubtful. A deep skill in sensing what may and may not be done. A gift if not for friendship at least for amicable association with other minds and with the interests of others.

And then, of purely human qualities there are yet more. The really good Senator must be a man of such sensitivity, a sensitivity not expressed by mere softness, as to be able to perceive those odd surges of feeling that mysteriously move among men generally, sometimes informing and sometimes obscuring the true meaning of issues before the Senate. He need not be particularly skilled in every kind of human relationship but this instinct of high discrimination is indispensable. It is, sometimes, the only quality that stands athwart hysterical action.

Then he must have a considerable essential ardor for life, an *élan vital* that is constant if not necessarily intense, to survive in a trying and hazardous way of life. This was the sort of quality that enabled Mr. Truman, an old Senate man,

117

to go doggedly forward in 1948, refusing to be discouraged, while associates on his very campaign train were quite certain that he was finished. It was the quality that permitted Senator Taft, dying a rushing death from cancer, to go on working to the end, accomplishing in the weeks of his last illness more than he had accomplished before.

It was the quality that caused a Kerr of Oklahoma to stand alone day after day in the Institution, in the extraordinary period immediately after Mr. Truman's recall of General MacArthur from Far Eastern command, to defend the right of a civilian President to act as he had acted. It appeared for a time then that a considerable part of the country, and perhaps even a majority, had forgotten the great democratic principle of civil control of the military.

Requisite, too, is a kind of *inner* detachment and disinterestedness, a thing found fairly often in the most ordinarily partisan of men, in political "machines" indeed as well as in the Institution itself. A good Senator cannot become so emotionally involved with his issues as to lose his perspective; an outer emotionalism is all right, in speaking for example, but an inner emotionalism will tend to paralyze the mind in a place where this is fatal. This is why liberal movements, by the way, are better led by men of objective humor and interior detachment than by the zealots whose conviction may burn away their common sense, except in the rare and desperate cases of history.

And the quality of disinterestedness does not mean, of

118

course, a lack of concern in what is afoot; very far from it. The late Senator Brien McMahon of Connecticut was as hard and as acute a practical partisan as the Senate is likely to see. In the meetings of the Senate Democratic Policy Committee, of which he was a member, there was from him never a counsel other than the counsel of partisan attack— except on some matters.

When the Atomic Age burst upon the world with the holocausts of Hiroshima and Nagasaki, there opened before the United States one of the greatest political dilemmas— quite apart from the numberless dilemmas loosed in other aspects of life—since its founding. Here was a weapon of unexampled ferocity—and a material of unguessable benign potential. How should it be controlled? The Executive Branch of the United States Government, thinking of the need for secrecy and thinking of the horror that had to be contained, was ready to put the whole of the enterprise under what would have amounted to a garrison control by the military.

It was McMahon of Connecticut, a man who had elbowed his way to the top and a man who would have been quite at home in the most realistic political ward meeting in the United States, who now displayed the truly sensitive and perceptive mind, the mind of a basic disinterestedness. He saw at once where total military control, of a Thing more powerful than ever before conceived, might lead. In the Senate he stormed and fought, at first with little assistance, for the principle of civilian control that led at last to the establishment of the Atomic Energy Commission.

And at a lesser though entirely valid level of his life as a man of the Institution, he arranged at the same time to become the chairman of the Joint Congressional Committee now set up to supervise the Commission itself.

X

CRIME

AND PUNISHMENT

THE STANDARD of proper conduct for a Senator is about what the Institution says it is—at a given time, in a given circumstance and with regard to a given member. The rules are made to be observed; but then again they are made to be broken by some men sometimes. It is a place, so protected as it is both by the Constitution and old custom, where privilege in personal behavior is high and inhibitions on personal behavior are very rare. The easiest and somewhat oversimplified way to express the real situation is simply to say that the great ones do about as they please, short of action so outrageous as not possibly to be overlooked. The rest, except for the unhappy few in any session who somehow are not acceptable at all, can in the vulgar phrase get away with *almost* anything so long as it is not directed against anybody in the Inner Club.

For the Senate honors and elevates age and personality as does no other place in government. And, honoring age, it does not merely tolerate but actually enjoys the crotchets of highly individualistic men.

It is possible for one of the seniors, on almost any day when he may feel of a mind, to give one of the juniors such a dressing down, in spirit, as a top sergeant may give to a recruit—though in much more orotund phraseology. Old Senator Connally of Texas, to recall such an incident, once addressed himself for half an hour to the alleged demerits of Senator Homer Ferguson of Michigan in terms hardly less wounding than blows in the face. Ferguson, who through his two terms never quite understoood the Senate, notwithstanding his possession of certain sterling qualities like persistence and doggedness, had been annoying many in the place by what seemed to be his notion that he was a sort of self-convoked one-man caucus for moral reform. He had most explicitly been annoying Connally.

Specifically, Ferguson had been attacking certain of the official acts of another eminent Texan, Tom C. Clark, then Attorney General and now a Justice of the Supreme Court of the United States.

Though there is a rule that says one member must not question the motives of another, Connally, long before he had at last been gently and apologetically called to order, had to the non-Senatorial ear rather thoroughly explored and condemned nearly all of Ferguson's motives. He had, for illustration, at one point observed, in a strident bellow flung into the face of the Senator from Michigan: "Everything he touches is covered with the vomit of his spleen!"

All the same, this expression, harsh though it was, was the expression of an especially favored Senate type. It was directed at a member, Ferguson, who had at the time been constituting himself, for all that he was a comparative newcomer, as a kind of personal Senate grand jury. Too, Connally was—simply Connally; and who did not cherish the "old man"? And finally it is difficult, in this place so devoted to debate, for the Senate to think of disciplining a member for what he *says*. The Constitution guarantees that for what he says here he may not be "questioned" elsewhere; the Senate has not been behindhand in exploiting that privilege.

Still, there *is* a line of limit—though it is a moving line and never a fixed one and there may be many days and many sets of facts in which it is absent altogether—as to what is proper conduct in the Senate and what qualifies a man to sit or continue to sit there. (The Institution of course by the Constitution is exclusively the judge of the qualifications of its own members, once the States have chosen those members.)

History's record of the various proceedings taken against offending members makes the Senate far from a hanging judge, though the verdict has not *always* been acquittal. In 1850 Senators Foote of Mississippi and Benton of Missouri got into a little incident that might have seemed un-Senatorial. When Benton strode toward Foote's seat with battle in his eye Foote drew and cocked a pistol and other members had to intervene to prevent bloodshed. The outcome: a committee report that it was all quite deplorable and a warning that must "not be unheeded in the future."

In 1902 Senators Tillman and McLaurin, colleagues from South Carolina, had a fist fight on the Senate floor and both were at first "declared to be in contempt of the Senate." Each apologized, each was then censured "For breach of the privileges and dignity of this body," and that was the end of it.

Expulsions from the Senate, a penalty it is able to put into effect by two-thirds vote, have been extremely rare, and when they have occurred at all action has been based on what amounted to nothing less than violation of criminal laws. Even then the case for the defense, so to speak, has usually fared better than that for the prosecution. In 1807 Senator Smith of Ohio avoided expulsion on the roll call by one vote even after he had been indicted in Federal Court for treason, though he resigned before the year was out.

(A Southern Senator and true Senate type, Pinckney, saved Smith's seat; he attacked the investigating committee's report as not according to due process.)

As to the Senators from the South on the eve of the War Between the States, the Institution moved with the greatest delicacy. When Jefferson Davis, then a Senator from Mississippi, and the others announced the secession of their States and left the chamber, an attempt was made by the more belligerent Northerners to have their names stricken from the roll call. This the Senate refused to do. Instead, ten days after the inauguration of Lincoln as President, it passed a resolution simply stating that since the seats of Davis and the others had "become vacant . . . the Secretary be directed to omit their names respectively from the roll."

An effort to expel Senator Lazarus W. Powell of the Border State of Kentucky, for presiding over a pro-Southern rally in which it was resolved that the North "was invading" the South, failed when the Judiciary Committee held: ". . . He is entitled to his own opinions, and no man is to be expelled from this body because he disagrees with others in opinion." At the same time, Senators Trusten Polk and

125

Waldo Johnson of Missouri were expelled on the finding that they had participated in *acts* against the Union.

Indeed, the whole history of the Institution shows this general view of Senatorial conduct: First, a strong disinclination to proceed at all against *any* Senator. Second, an effort, in measuring behavior, not to equate offensive thought and language with offensive and palpable *acts*.

It was this tradition that lay at the bottom of the Senate's long hesitation before it dealt with Senator Joseph R. McCarthy of Wisconsin, though political timidity had its place. And when, in December of 1954, he was at length condemned by a vote of 67 to 22, it was for purely *Senatorial* offenses and not at all for what his critics in the public had long charged against him—an attack on the Bill of Rights, a habit of accusation without proof, a campaign of divisiveness affecting the whole of the Republic, a denial of the oldest traditions of the English-speaking heritage. He was in fact tried not for intellectual crime against the people and the Republic (though this was the charge really debated pro and con among the public) but wholly for his conduct concerning the *Institution*. The scene inside was vastly removed from the scene outside. It was not the hostile press and public that brought McCarthy to his accounting. It was not the Eisenhower Administration. It was not the Republican party, though clearly seeing as it did that he was in a political sense ultimately the responsibility of that party.

126

It was the Institution that finally brought him to book—an Institution led, as always in these supreme crises involving its real life, by its Senate types of the Inner Club.

In the summer of 1954 the scattered liberal forces of the Senate, through Flanders of Vermont among the Republicans and Fulbright of Arkansas among the Democrats, began moving insistently for action to discipline McCarthy. The heart of their proposals, however worthy and however brave, was not truly *Senatorial*. Though McCarthy's mere name had been a public controversy for four years, the instinct of the Senate remained resolved upon avoiding the precipitate—and the purpose of Flanders and Fulbright actually was to condemn him out of hand. This, however forthright, was not at all to the taste of the great majority, which looked for guidance to the Senate types.

These were greatly concerned, first, not to attempt any action against McCarthy without a formal hearing, and, second, not to attempt anything in any case without the ultimate in due deliberation. They did not forget that this was only the third time in 165 years that the Institution had considered a censure of one of its members.

There was, moreover, the important fact that a Congressional election was coming in the autumn and the proprieties —and secondarily the careers of some nervous members then up for re-election—would best be served by deferring the great issue until the campaigning session had passed. At length, therefore, it was agreed that the Senate should proceed at once to appoint a select committee of inquiry, which would hold its hearings during the campaign season. The Senate itself would return in November to deliver the final judgment.

What was not generally understood then was the important fact that on the day that the Senate made provision for this select committee it made all but inevitable the eventual comdemnation of Senator McCarthy. This moral certainty lay in a number of complicated reasons. In the first place, it was perfectly obvious to all who understood the movement of general thought within the place that a substantial majority of those who ultimately must try him knew already in their own intimate experience, before so much as a word of testimony had been taken, that McCarthy demonstrably and repeatedly had been guilty of conduct prejudicial to the good name of the Senate.

In the second place, the Senate being the Senate, the decision to proceed with the establishment of the select committee in itself amounted to a general unspoken acceptance that a prima facie case had already been made against McCarthy. In the third place, it was clear that the Senate types, in the subtle and mysterious way that these things are communicated, had already made an essential judgment that he had gone too far.

Finally, and most conclusive, there was the nature of the personnel of the select committee as it was selected by the Democratic and Republican Senate leaders, Senators Johnson of Texas and Knowland of California. It was the character and the individual circumstances of these judges that made the outcome foregone. The chairman, Arthur V. Watkins of Utah, was in profession a profoundly correct lawyer, in politics a "regular" Republican loyal to the Eisenhower Administration that McCarthy was endangering, and in moral life an almost painfully ethical Mormon. Thin, gray, sternly upright, shy and ascetic, looking out upon his fellows from glittering rimless glasses, he had several times before in his career shown the white-faced courage of the gentle and timid man.

He had, moreover, a record for a kind of glacial fairness and cold objectivity, and a matchless general respectability. He was the kind of a man to whom Senator Knowland once said he would willingly entrust his own life. He was, in a word, the perfect type figure of one of the Senate's moods, its mood of judgment. And under the parsonical manner there was steel.

His senior committee colleague on the Democratic side, Senator Edwin C. Johnson of Colorado, was a worthy vis-à-vis. Johnson, who later gave up his Senatorial career to become Governor of Colorado (for the sole and simple reason that his wife disliked Washington life) was as influential inside the Institution as he was little known or noted outside it. He had developed a personal legend of an almost supernatural political skill. He was almost wholly unpartisan in important senses; about as many Republicans

129

as Democrats had been his habitual backers in Colorado and on many routine matters he worked in perfectly open harness with his Republican colleague, Senator Millikin. Edwin Johnson, moreover, had the innate quality of judgment and, even more vitally, the quality of absolute political fearlessness past a certain point. His slow, ruminative, plodding mind, innocent of any trace of brilliance and alive with memories of Senate tradition, matched his powerful, controlled, bearlike body. He was a man slow to wrath as he was slow to decision; but once a conviction had lodged in his head no possible intimidating pressure could knock it out.

Next in hierarchical order on the select committee on the Republican side there came Senator Frank Carlson of Kansas, a good "Eisenhower man," a farmer, a stockman, a Baptist, a second-generation American of Swedish stock. Again a slow, careful, peaceful but incorruptible man. And again a member more powerful in internal Senate affairs than on external issues before that body.

Then there was, to complete the Republican panel, Senator Francis Case of South Dakota, a dry, somewhat pedantic, small, bald, intense man, who was nowhere near the Inner Club and was the one member of the select committee to weaken after it had brought in its counts against McCarthy. Case, a teetotaler and the son of a retired Methodist minister, measurably retreated from the strictures he had first endorsed when the McCarthy affair came to the floor for a final decision.

130

Ed Johnson's Democratic colleagues on the committee were both Southerners and both members in good standing of the Inner Club, Ervin of North Carolina and Stennis of Mississippi. Both had judicial backgrounds. Both were men of known moderation of view. Both were traditional "Senate men," and both were men of established political courage.

This, then, was the phalanx of judgment that confronted McCarthy. Not a man on the select committee was nationally prominent as it began its deliberations; but not a man on it, with the exception of Case, lacked great distinction *inside* the Institution. From the start, they saw their duty in this light: They were not to try McCarthy because of what he had done *so far as the public was concerned.* They were not trying McCarthy for what he had done or said or not said in what he called his "fight on Communism." They were not trying McCarthy as a disruptive influence on a political party, the Republican party. They were not trying him for irresponsibility as a public official. They were not even trying him for his privilege to sit in the Senate.

In the real sense, as they actually viewed the business, the public was not involved in their duties, except in so far as the public was concerned in the kind of place the Senate was. "We realize," said Watkins, when the hearings opened, "that *the United States Senate* is on trial. . . ."

It is only in this context of the underlying reality, as the Institution appreciated it, that the whole of the proceeding can be truly understood. It wars not a trial in the commonly

131

understood meaning at all; the judges clearly and inevitably had prior opinions, for day after day they had all sat with McCarthy. They were not hearing an action at law; they were determining simply the *degree* that a member had transgressed the rules, written or not, and the spirit of the club to which he belonged.

Thus it was that the findings of the select committee seemed to many so strangely irrelevant—irrelevant alike to those in the public who had all but canonized their swarthy and muscular hero, McCarthy, and to those whose firmest conviction was that his had been a truly historic crime.

And, indeed, if the matter be viewed in this light, what an odd indictment it was!

"Resolved, that the Senator from Wisconsin, Mr. McCarthy, failed to cooperate with the Subcommittee on Privileges and Elections of the Senate Committee on Rules and Administration in clearing up matters which concerned his conduct as a Senator and affected the honor of the Senate and, instead, repeatedly abused the subcommittee and its members who were trying to carry on their assigned duties, thereby obstructing the Constitutional processes of the Senate; and that this conduct of the Senator from Wisconsin, Mr. McCarthy, is contrary to Senatorial traditions and is hereby condemned.

"The Senator from Wisconsin, Mr. McCarthy, acted contrary to Senatorial ethics and tended to bring the Senate into dishonor and disrepute, to obstruct the Constitutional processes of the Senate, and to impair its dignity. . . ."

Reflecting back upon the harsh days of "McCarthyism," upon the bitterness of a divided country, upon all that in the general sense was here involved, had the majestic mountain, the Senate, not brought forth a very small mouse indeed? In that sense, possibly yes. But as the Institution sees it, not at all.

For the Senate never conceded that this was a truly *public* problem; it was a *Senate* problem and the Senate moved in its way to solve it. It was, on its face, a solution that left much unresolved. Untouched, in theory, was McCarthy's power there. His right to vote, to remain on the very committee where the Institution had found he had worked his harm—all these too remained. But, ostensibly unpunished though he was, there was real and lasting punishment. A door, quite unseen but quite heavy, had been shut before him. He might well remain a great power to a substantial minority in his own party and elsewhere. But in the Institution he was a power no longer.

For again the Senate has its ways, and one of these was illustrated in the post-condemnation days. Again and again when McCarthy rose to speak there was in the chamber that rarest of all demonstrations, a demonstration of conscious disorder and inattention. Tolerance is a long rope here, a very long one. But, give a man enough rope . . .

XI

PRESSURES

ON SENATORS

A SENATOR of the United States is an ambulant converging point for pressures and counter-pressures of high, medium and low purposes. The variety and complexity and severity of these pressures will largely be determined by the economic nature, the size and degree of homogeneity of his state. The one absolutely common factor of the business is that no member of the Senate, however well favored by circumstance, can wholly escape them and that they seem to grow and to rise in intensity with the passage of time.

Indeed it is a fact that the Institution, which is a national body only after it is a body of the States and the sections, is if anything progressively less national in its approach to most affairs. This is the odd state of things even as the country itself becomes more and more bound into a unit by its extraordinarily efficient systems of communications and by the steady growth of what might be called national as distinguished from local or sectional industry. Big Business (motors, steel, transport, the press and so on) is increasingly centralized in the sense of its ultimate control through mergers, while it is increasingly decentralized at the point of production by the rise in many new areas of satellite plants and other operating facilities. The Senate at the same time is increasingly engaged upon the protection of what is primarily local or sectional in economic life.

All this is a preface to a consideration of one, but not necessarily the principal one, of the pressures upon individual members and on the Institution itself, the pressure of economic interest. This pressure is of course a singular term for a great pluralism of winds and cross-winds. There is in the Senate no possibility of finding and fixing a *single*

national economic interest, for this is a deliberately and un-
changeably disparate place where unity in such an area
of life is not only unacceptable but is consciously fought.

For an example, it seems to me that the generality of the
national interest undoubtedly has been served by the tariff-
cutting policies formulated by Cordell Hull in the Reciprocal
Trade Program. At all events, this program increasingly
is being supported by truly *national* Big Business; recall for
example, that young Henry Ford has done important work
for the principle of lower tariffs and that much of what is
called "Wall Street" has for years been on the same side
of the case. Parenthetically, the consequence has been that
a pro-world-trade man like Eisenhower (and Willkie and
Dewey before him) had a far higher degree of backing
from the truly rich and industrially powerful than the late
Taft or almost any other typically Senate man could ever
have marshaled.

Nevertheless, and in spite of what might fairly be called a
general acceptance *nationally* by both parties of the desirability of continuing the Hull policy, the Senate in the
Eighty-fourth Congress continued that program only at the
cost of great dilutions of the principle wrung from the lower-
tariff forces who in the country as a whole were incomparably more powerful than they were in the Institution.
These concessions offered a good view of an instance where
many local and sectional interests happened to coincide and
so drew together a group of Senators large enough to insist

upon the various protectionist hedges that found their way into the ultimate bill. For an illustration, the greatest of the oil States, Texas, is also a part of the section where free-trade sentiment historically has been greatest, the South. But here vital Texas interests, and vital Louisiana interests for that matter, found some common purpose with the vital interests of small-manufacturing States elsewhere.

This was an instance where pressures on Senators were fortuitously rationalized by circumstances; more often than not this is anything but the state of affairs. There are many times when pressures and counter-pressures not only can never be eased and balanced off but actually run dead against each other with almost equal weight and velocity. Where, for example, is the dominant pressure for the Senators from New York when taxes on oleomargarine are on the agenda? The millions of consumers in Metropolitan New York will not, to the degree that they are conscious of the issue, care at all for these taxes. But the most basic industry in upstate New York is the production of milk. To dairymen oleo is an unpleasant product indeed.

Again, in Iowa the packinghouse industry of the cities is fundamentally at cross-purpose with the hopes of the rural cattle-feeding industry; the one wants the price of steers for slaughter to be reasonably low and the other of course wants it to be high.

Economic pressure, however, is only the beginning for a Senator. In the more intimate sense there is the pressure of

138

constituents, of lobbies, of his own party and of the White House.

The constituents' pressures are by definition almost in-finitely varied. To adjust matters with the Veterans Admin-istration, whose letters about life-insurance policies often are in a bureaucratese so staggeringly impenetrable as to make Pentagon language seem the most limpid of prose. To get a friend a Government job or a son a transfer in the military services. To intervene with the Army not to close the hospital on which Beeville has so depended. To insist that the Department of Agriculture reinstruct the local repre-sentative about the assistance he is giving to digging the field pond. To do a thousand things for *individuals* at war, justly or not, with a distant administrative bureaucracy necessarily seeking a conformity of operation and approach that appeals neither to those individuals nor to the Senator himself. To insist, on a higher level of appeal, that the Senator vote this way or that way on great issues. And so on.

This sort of constituent pressure, except for the last illus-trated, is not itself a particularly wearing thing on a member of the Senate, for he usually has in his office one or more experts in "contacting" the Federal agencies, and sometimes he even has an expert whose main function is simply to smell out general opinion in the home State—preliminary to surveys by the old master.

The pressure on Senatorial voting, however, is quite a different matter; it cannot possibly be left to the responsibility of any office expert. Men respond to it—and on emotional issues like McCarthyism or the military draft it reaches a profound pitch—as is their individual bent. Some pretend at least to be deeply concerned with each communication. Others, the Senate types particularly, have long since made their philosophy of dealing with pressure mail. They decline to rate it by the pound, having seen many a postcard campaign couched in language of appeal or threat. And if they are bent on a contrary course they avoid any *lengthy* explanation or anything approaching servile apology for their action. In the Institution all explanation is to be avoided if at all possible (for a defensive position is rarely wise) and if explanation there must be it is as laconic as possible. And counter-attack is sometimes employed. Senator Albert Gore of Tennessee, hard-pressed on the telephone by a determined lady backer of the Bricker Amendment to limit the treaty-making power of the Presidency, took part in this colloquy:

Constituent: "I *demand* to know, Senator, how you stand on the Bricker Amendment."

Gore, in his awareness first that "the Bricker Amendment" was so complicated as not truly to be understood by one-twentieth of the public and second that at least seven variants of it were then extant: "*Which* Bricker Amendment, Ma'am?"

Indeed, constituent pressure cannot be examined usefully without dealing with some of the endless qualifications concerning it. A Senator from a State where a man

140

owes election primarily to a powerful party organization, say Rhode Island, rarely jumps at any constituent whip. Old Senator Theodore Francis Green of that State, rich, aristocratic and entrenched, was one of the original accusers of Senator McCarthy back in the days of the investigation made of some of his charges by the Tydings Committee.

Green, who held McCarthy in angry and open contempt, never for a moment pretended to any objectivity in the matter and quickly fell afoul of the McCarthyites of his State. At one point shoals of postcards, some of them quite vile, descended upon the old gentleman, and one day he was showing some samples to me. They were full, among other things, of the direst threats upon his political life, and I asked: "What about all these, Senator?"

"Odd, disgusting little things, aren't they?" he said in a bored, fastidious drawl, using the very end of his fingernail to flick his communications into the wastebasket. That closed the subject with him.

Another Senator operating in another set of basic facts, however, will of course respond in quite another way, though the technique of attempting to *force* any member of the Senate to do a certain thing or accept a certain idea is almost certain to fail.

Speaking generally, constituent pressure is rarely the *cause* of any Senator's action, for if it is powerful enough to be all-persuasive it can come in only one of two ways: It emanates from bread-and-butter interest of his State so unarguably

141

fundamental to its welfare as to make it clearly unnecessary to implore the member to act promptly and strongly for a local interest quite indistinguishable from his own. Or it, this kind of pressure, arises from the deepest moral or spiritual or social convictions and impulsions of the State, its whole way of life. Who, for an illustration, would suppose it would be necessary to insist upon support for reasonably generous immigration policies from almost any Senator conceivably capable of election from a State like New York? A member of the Institution, in short, is in all the most important ways very like his State, and literally a living part of it, long before he reaches Washington.

Then, there is the pressure from lobbies and lobbyists. The devil image long associated with such activities has been fading for years, with a general rise in political understanding. It is not necessary, therefore, to dwell long on the now generally accepted facts that there is no inherent evil in lobbying, that much of it serves a good purpose, and that most of it has become as respectable as running a Chamber of Commerce—and certainly a good deal less dull.

Again, however, truly effective lobbying usually comes in the ways that truly effective constituent pressure comes— that is, not so much shrill advocacy for a course of Senatorial action as in assisting already sympathetic Senators in obtaining that action. Many professional political observers, perhaps using different measures, offer many different answers to the question as to which is the most effective of all lobbies. My own experience has suggested that the most triumphant lobby of all in the defensive sense—in maintaining roughly the *status quo*—is that of the physicians in the American Medical Association. The fact is that for a generation the Senate has shied away from or actively rejected innovations in the field of public health that would be regarded as quite tame and far from desperately "socialistic" in the similar field of education.

Among the probable reasons for this success of the medicos with the Institution is that at heart it is more sympathetic to professional men than to any other class except another quite traditional one, the farmers. Another is the strong, half-instinctive belief among Senators that doctors will (or ought to) tend to express the *suitable* and lasting attitudes of a community rather than the unsuitable and the transitory. Finally, there is a Senatorial view, factual or founded on legend as it may be, that doctors are more influential than all others (except possibly priests in a Catholic area) in developing important public thought. (A genuine test of this theory would be interesting. It probably arises from the tireless propaganda of physicians themselves.)

As to affirmative lobbying, where the end is to *change* things and to make gains for groups of people, the farm lobby is unquestionably the strongest of the field. Again, however, this is no case of operating with slinky women, whiskey or even the propaganda taradiddle now usually called hucksterism. The farm-State Senator usually has no

143

need whatever to be convinced; the representatives of the farm organizations meet with him not as pleading favor seekers but as members of a fifth estate which he recognizes in the most genuine sense of that term.

Labor, too, has an able lobby; but here, too, it would be quite unwise to imagine a brutal and heavy-handed series of orders issuing from labor organizers to scared "politicians" in the Senate. The attitude of a Murray of Montana or a Kilgore of West Virginia will be as unashamedly pro-labor, without the slightest hint of dissimulation or evasion, as was the pro-business attitude of old Boies Penrose of Pennsylvania. Labor's lobby operates in the full light of day, from offices that are nothing less than grand, and staffed with able, professional personnel who but for differing private convictions could as well work for the National Association of Manufacturers.

The lobbies for business are, on the whole, both less effective and less well known than those for labor and the farmers. Editorialists who are in great anxiety about the slightly lesser activity of the business lobby should not for a moment feel, however, that all is lost. "Business" in the Institution remains a clearer concept than does "labor", and business has measurably less need for lobbyists in force.

Then there are other lobbies, some rather less open than those thus far described and some far less open. The various forms of transportation maintain lobbyists of various kinds. The point is admittedly speculative and not subject to docu-

144

mented proof, but the bystander's impression is that in the newest of the transportation industries, the airlines, the representatives of the trade are certainly more energetic and possibly a good deal more heavy-handed than those for the railroads and the buses.

All this complex of known lobbying—ranging from the perfectly frank and useful kind of the really big national lobbies to the somewhat less frank but rarely sinister kinds—achieves debatable results. It is, here as elsewhere, true that in order usefully and long to influence the Senate there are absolutely no substitutes for both good faith and a good case.

Among the most vehement of all lobbyists are those who, officially or by self-appointment, speak for "patriotic organizations," some of which are honorably and incontestably that and others which do not necessarily fall into that exact category. These deal almost wholly in emotional and fringe issues—"fringe" in the sense that they are issues not likely to come to much in the way of Senatorial action. They make, taking them altogether, almost no real impression on the Senate. For, however high may be their good faith, their varying cases are almost always poor to bad.

Many no doubt will recall, as fresh in mind, the lobbying scandals attached in 1956 to the bill to free natural gas producers from direct Federal controls—the bill vetoed by President Eisenhower because though he liked its objective he did not like the way it had passed.

There was lobbying here, all right, and plenty of it—but it was on two sides. For many public utilities were in this case quite as actively opposed to the bill as were the consumer groups. What made this a noteworthy incident was not the essential nature of the case—it was fundamentally simply a case where State interest was colliding with State interest, the interest of the gas-producing States against the interest of the consumer States.

No; in this case the business became a *cause célèbre* because of the ineptitude of gas lobbyists who went about offering cash campaign contributions to various Senators about the time the decisive vote on the gas bill was to be expected.

The subsequent clear disinclination of the Senate patriarchs to rush into any investigation of the affair was, again, not a clear example of what many thought to be simply the power of evil. The facts are (a) that all but a few Senators must depend on some major source of campaign contributions, be it Big Business or Big Labor, and (b) that the conservative Democrats have no reliable corporate source save the oil and gas industry. The general run of the Republicans, on the other hand, have a variety of such corporate sources; the liberal Democrats have a rich (and again quite proper) source in the labor organizations.

The patriarchs, in short, were prepared to see an investigation of *all* sources of campaign contributions, but not an inquiry confined largely to this one source.

What went on here was traditional lobbying, in this case

146

uglied up by activities more foolish then corrupt. And where did it occur? Not, literally, in the lobbies of the Senate chamber, for these are reserved to members and ex-members; but rather in Senatorial offices and carpeted corridors and all about Washington. Lobbyists also sat and intently watched proceedings from the public Senate galleries—as they did in about equal numbers a week or so later when a bill allocating sugar quotas was up for debate.

To set the scene, incidentally, let me describe the Senate chamber itself, as it exists today and will long exist. To begin with, it is a large, cool, conservatively decorated rectangle on the second floor of the west side of the Capitol, overlooking Union Station, a rather grand Capitol plaza—and some of the most intractable slums in Washington. The presiding officer—the Vice-President of the United States or his alternate, the president pro tem of the Senate—sits upon a raised but not especially elegant dais, flanked just below by the Senate parliamentarian, the reading clerk and perhaps by a few blue-suited page boys lolling about waiting for some member to snap his fingers.

To the presiding officer's left, as he looks down from his comparative eminence upon an assembly of men who pay him no more attention than need be, sits the Republican side of the Senate. To his right, across a narrow aisle, sits the Democratic side.

Directly ahead of the presiding officer and in the far background is the back door to the chamber. Flanking it on either side are doors leading to the two Senate lounges—one for the Republicans and one for the Democrats. Another word for these lounges is cloakrooms. It is here that the partisans are entrenched, like men in a good club, from all save their fellows and their employees, in the privacy of their party's home within the Senate. Other exits from the chamber lead to a gilded and massive room called "the President's Room" and to a large corridor-waiting room. In the first of these rooms, "the President's Room," Senators meet with members of the press. (One sends in a member of the Senate staff and asks for Senator So-and-So. If he is available and in the mood he comes out to "the President's Room.") The other and larger room is for the public—including lobbyists (who may also be constituents) and simply constituents. There is nothing clandestine about it all; meetings here are as matter-of-fact as any business meeting in any conference room of any corporation office. Here, among other places, the lobbyists actually lobby. They are for the most part lawyers; and of late years a large percentage of them are ex-New Deal or Fair Deal officials and bureaucrats jousting now with the older, corporation-lawyer kind of lobbyist. The incidence of paunches among these people is about as high as would be found in any other profession; no higher, so far as one has noticed.

Finally, there are the purely personal and self-designated lobbyists who haunt the Senate, seeking a few minutes at committee meetings here or there to testify with matchless verve on almost any subject that comes to mind. Some of these are the greatest of nuisances—and one or two would seem to a layman to be clearly certifiable. It is, nevertheless, not the least of the Institution's glories that these odd characters, who would be escorted at once from any judicial proceeding in the land and who never in the world would be allowed to approach even a minor official in the Executive Department, can have their solemn hearing in this place.

A very considerable space of the time of the Senate Foreign Relations Committee, the most powerful legislative agent in all the world, has been given over to these hapless characters, one of whom on each and every occasion flies out at all present but for all that has never felt on her shoulder any touch more hostile than the gently restraining hand of a Senate guard.

Lobbies, in sum, are influential for what they *are* and not for what they do. No one could properly describe their pressures on a Senator as either unbearable or clearly harmful.

The pressure of a Senator's national party on him is a somewhat different matter. Its effectiveness varies from the substantially non-existent in the case, say, of Senator Eastland of Mississippi, who has no need whatever of the Democratic National Committee, to the considerable in the case of any Senator from a close two-party State who is up for re-election. This latter member of the Institution must make *some* contact with his national organization, especially at times such as these, but how close the contact must be is always in doubt

149

and the essential seniority of the Senator to the second party to the communication, the national party, is rarely in doubt at all.

The truth is that a *party* rarely can put truly effective pressure on *any* Senator; though a powerful and popular Presidential head of that party can do so, at rare times. Putting the thing more concretely, the national party organization will greatly hope that a sitting Senator will, in his campaign for re-election, adopt its general political attitudes.

It will offer him much assistance, some of it valuable and all of it free, with this hope in mind, but it will rarely ever withdraw this assistance even if he takes a strictly lone-wolf political position. In 1954 not only the regular Republican organization but the avowedly non-partisan Citizens for Eisenhower found it possible to give total endorsement to a Senatorial candidate in Illinois, Joseph Meek, whose whole political philosophy could hardly have been more at variance with both the national Republican official line and that of President Eisenhower himself.

The Senate, for its part, is most of the time rather indifferent to what the national party organizations believe and desire, and so, in their hearts, are at least a majority of its members. One "Democratic" Senator reaching the chamber from the 1952 elections, Price Daniel of Texas, had campaigned for, spoken privately for, and voted for the Republican candidate for President.

The Democratic National Committee, which read out of

the party a national committeeman from Texas for a similar but lesser apostasy, was in timorous hope that Daniel would be chastised by the Senate Democrats. Instead, they took him instantly and without the slightest discussion or comment into the Democratic fold.

No President, no party organization, no constituents, lobby or any other force, can put upon the Institution sufficient pressures to cause it to do what it did not want to do in the first place, *so long as it regards the issue involved as truly fundamental and so long as it regards itself as the last proper place for resolving that issue.*

It is not, in all times and circumstances, incorruptible. And it is not, at any time, incapable of disservice to the country and grave error. But that grave error, when it occurs, will be its own.

151

XII

THE PRESSURES

FROM SENATORS

WHILE the pressures *on* Senators are well known and have certain modified effects already described, the pressures *from* Senators are in fact more intensive, more effective and

153

far less recognized by the public for what they are.

The Institution is subjected to many eddying currents of thought and hope; but it sends out more than it receives. The Senate's impact on other political organisms and indeed on national life as a whole is far greater than is their combined impact on it. From about the middle of the second term of Franklin D. Roosevelt through the whole of the tenure of Harry S. Truman the Senate exercised a recurring veto over the most liberal domestic policies of two Presidents holding fairly clear mandates from a majority of the people of the United States.

In all of that time it is extremely unlikely that any member of the Institution, or even any hypothetical member miraculously embodying in his single person the most attractive of the attributes of half a dozen of his leading colleagues, could have given either of these Presidents any sort of a contest for popular approval.

From about the onset of the Cold War to the enigmatic turn of affairs some eight years later that saw the West entering conversations with the world Communists, the Senate exercised a recurring veto over much that American administrations would have *liked* to do, if not what they actually attempted to do in foreign policy. In none of this period, and certainly not in its latter part when the President involved was Eisenhower, would the Senate have dared put its view of the proper policy to the ultimate test before the national jury of the aggregate of the voters.

154

Nevertheless, these views—which in principle equated negotiation with appeasement and involved the Institution's unspoken conviction that there could be no honorable solution between the two worlds short of a war that few wanted —in general prevailed for nearly a decade.

Just so with the Institution's convictions as to what was impermissible in the domestic programs of both Roosevelt and Truman. It is true that the outbreak of the Second World War is often considered to bear responsibility for the failure of the ultimate aspects of Mr. Roosevelt's New Deal. The point is debatable at best; the whole history of the last years of qualified national peace before Pearl Harbor indicates to me at least that the Senate would have halted Mr. Roosevelt in any case.

Certainly it halted Mr. Truman, and though it may be argued that Mr. Truman was no Roosevelt it must be conceded that all the same he obtained for his course a popular approval in 1948 that was as impressive as it was unexpected.

At all events, this case is confined to the observation that for whatever reasons one wishes at the moment to ascribe, the true fact is that in both these acute periods in modern national history the Institution successfully interposed itself against the operation of apparent popular will and of unquestioned Presidential will. As it did so it illustrated the most subtle kind of all Senatorial pressures.

This is the pressure that the Senate is able to exert, from the safest and most fortified political lodgment in the United

States, not only against *actions* by the Executive but in some instances even against its active *contemplation* of actions. This form of veto, call it retroactive or call it latent, can be exercised with or without the assistance of powerful persons and organizations in the non-political community.

In so often saying "no" in the thirties and forties to the more advanced domestic innovations of Presidents Roosevelt and Truman the Institution had of course the active and vehement support of the most influential part of the press and allied agencies. But in saying "no" to *all* the provisional plans of the Truman Administration to make some accommodation before Korea with the fact of Communist control of the China mainland, and in saying for two years precisely the same to the similar plans of the Eisenhower Administration, the Institution was largely going it alone.

It was of course not wholly without outside support and help. All in all, however, it could not be said that the principal national agencies of non-political power were truly or deeply committed one way or another on the issue. Indeed, if they had a tentative view it tended toward the side of accommodation, as was in fact suggested in 1955 when the most responsible leaders of the press instantly treated the Eisenhower decision to go to Geneva with the utmost respect and sympathy.

(The Institution, in the meantime, had changed its mind. Indeed, as has previously been pointed out, its hierarchs initiated the idea of Geneva and encouraged the President to take it up.)

But the purpose here is to explain the way these oddly powerful Senatorial pressures had worked so long and so well in both the areas of domestic and foreign policy. As to domestic matters, the business very nearly illustrates itself. Here, backed by the conservative forces of the country, the Senate had merely to appeal again and again to the past and to put upon the innovators the legitimate and heavy burden of the proof. It *did* use some of its more forthright means—its power over appropriations for one. But on the whole it had only to represent and endlessly to articulate nothing more palpable than a traditional point of view, and simply to refuse to act.

As to the foreign aspect of the thing the task was far harder and the opposition far more formidable. Here, in its fundamental resistance to change, and specifically to a change from adamancy to a certain softness toward the Communists, the Senate employed the basic weapons of one of its most puissant functions, the making not merely of propaganda but if need be of what might be called punitive propaganda.

Having reached the conclusion that the Iron Curtain defined a menace that was real indeed, and having been greatly influenced by the incomparable Churchill, the nearest British equivalent to a Senate type, the Senate took one of those strangely instinctive and quite unrecorded decisions of which it is capable. This was that the American Executive leadership had gravely underestimated Russian potential for aggression during and after the Second World War and that the *essential* purposes of American foreign policy had now best be formulated by the Institution itself. Involved of course was some considerable degree of distrust in a *particular* President, Mr. Truman. In the historic sense, however, what was more truly involved was the Senate's basic feeling of alienation from the Presidency as an institution in what it regarded as a period of a special kind of crisis. The Presidency, as the *Presidency*, was held to have failed in permitting this crisis to arise; the determination was that it should not now be allowed to fail again.

Thus there began to come into play the harshest, most efficacious—and the least defensible—of all the pressures of which the Senate is capable. Its Republican wing now set out upon a long and tortuous—and tortured—arraignment of both the wisdom and the *honor* of the actions of the Executive in the China crisis that at length had left the mainland in Communist hands. A harsh indictment, surpassingly ungenerous to the record of a whole nation—if a record largely made by an Executive, Mr. Truman—was now in countless hours of debate flung out from a great forum for all to read.

It opened as only a partisan legend or at the very best a bitter tale untested by any of the ordinary indispensable criteria for finding the true facts in a situation. But it ended, for millions of voters, as an established history in which some of the most eminent and honored personages of the United States were represented to be not mere fools and scoundrels but actually something akin to traitors. Chiang Kai-shek had been *deliberately* "sold out!" A vast Asian heartland had been consciously handed over to the Communists. The security of the United States and of all the West had been *purposely* endangered. Thus ran the extraordinary accusation.

And it became more than accusation because the Senate was in this case what it was. For the Democrats, upon whom one felt that the responsibility for rebuttal necessarily must rest, on the whole for some three years were strangely quiet.

Now and then one or another of them would rise to protest at a distortion of history of rarely exampled savagery, at a mystique of malevolence now being made into a statement of fact. Old Connally of Texas, harassed, ill and under hostile pressure from home, thundered as best he could, but very often he thundered alone. For the Democrats—most of the Democrats most of the time—had no stomach for a contest here with their Republican colleagues in the Institution.

Some, of course, were merely timid, but most of them were restrained for other and deeper reasons. Some of the greatest qualities of the Senate, its oneness and clannishness, its aloneness before the outer political organisms and the outer world, its instinctual drive for the supremacy of this integrious place—all these now were combined in such a

159

light as to shame that place before men of fairness everywhere.

For the Senate types had for the time become *only* Senate types; the large number of the good joined the small number of the bad in harshly promoting the claims of the Institution. Mr. Truman, old Senate man though he was, had few friends here at this juncture; not mainly because he was Mr. Truman but mainly because he was the *President* against whom the Senate was moving in its determination to capture here an *ultimate* power over foreign affairs that the Constitution had not given to it.

The identity, the personality, the essential worth of a military commander, however valuable otherwise, are not really at issue when he is at total war with another force.

And as this ultimate and punitive Senate pressure wrenched out of shape the history of a time of upheaval, collateral and equally punitive Senate pressures were set to work. This, the great home of absolute freedom of discussion, began not to be itself free of absolutism.

It allowed its vast propaganda powers to be turned, largely unrestrained, against all those everywhere—not merely at those in the combatant Executive Department in this great struggle but against political non-combatants everywhere— who did not share the Senate's interpretation of the events in Asia. There were distinguished and honorable exceptions. The most dedicated and advanced leader of the "hard" Asia policy line, Knowland of California, nevertheless by act and

160

example stood at every turn for free and unintimidated discussion—and it should not be forgotten that when the wheel had turned and the anti-"hard" policy liners came into control in the country those outside the Senate behaved toward him with none of the intellectual nobility that he had shown toward them. He considered a man could be anti-Chiang and yet not "subversive." They would not quite grant that he could be pro-Chiang and yet not "Formosa First."

Byrd of Virginia, far right-winger though he was, almost uniquely qualified though he was to dislike the Executive Department of Mr. Truman, gave with Knowland no hospitality to this distasteful and truly un-Senatorial clamor. Wiley of Wisconsin, pressed though he was by his colleague McCarthy and all the McCarthyites, did not forget the true character of the Institution. And there were others.

It was, for all that, a melancholy period in the life of the Senate, which, being very human, is very capable of wrong and folly against its own being and its own psyche. It was, however, even during some of this period, not wholly an ill record. For Senatorial pressures can be benign as well. It was primarily Senatorial pressure that caused the Eisenhower Administration to begin to re-examine the "security" programs to make certain that human rights were not to be freely sacrificed to national necessities that nevertheless could not properly be allowed to override the nation's reason for being.

It was Senatorial pressures, exerted in large part by men

who rarely agreed with him on political issues, that stood in the way in 1953 of an attempt among deeply partisan Republicans to assault not the judgment but the motives of Franklin Roosevelt in the Yalta Conference.

It is Senatorial pressures that for years similarly have been thrust in again and again against efforts by deeply partisan Democrats to suggest that Herbert Hoover was willfully lacking in compassion, and not merely politically inept, in the Great Depression.

The Institution, both parties of it, has not been willing in these cases to blacken the names and memories of men who were, after all, duly chosen Presidents of the United States of America.

The pressure that has sought to protect Mr. Hoover from mere calumny has been general and consistent. The pressure to protect Mr. Roosevelt's basic honor at Yalta was applied in the most specific possible way by Senate types among the Democrats, assisted, though not openly, by Senate types among the Republicans.

The Republican platform of 1952, in search for ways to make what turned out to be successful "nationality" appeals, primarily to the Poles, whose country indisputably fared badly at Yalta, roundly came out for a national repudiation of the Yalta agreements. The Senate Republicans, had they been merely *Republicans* and not in the last analysis members of the Institution, had the firmest of partisan precedent for going along with this: President Eisenhower himself had approved the platform. They were nevertheless not prepared to do so.

The Democratic Senate leader, Lyndon Johnson of Texas, was even less prepared to accept that sort of thing. He drew his party around him—the far right, the left, the center all together in this enterprise. He notified Secretary of State Dulles that the Democrats would accept a manifesto that *blamed only the Russians*—for violating the terms of Yalta and for enslaving peoples in Eastern Europe.

This turned out at length to be as far as the Senate itself would go, and when Republican extremists sought to harden the document, on which Johnson and Dulles had entered a gentleman's agreement, that was the end of the whole affair; nothing at all was done.

But I turn now to other aspects of pressure proceeding from rather than coming to a Senator. The pressure he employs on his constituents is usually interlinked and indistinguishable from the kind of pressure he puts on an Executive Department—that is, it is directed to high policy or actions.

As to his political party he is often a thorn, often a scourge and rarely an unmixed blessing. The essential independence of the place early colors his outlook, and in consequence he is far readier to lead his party organizations than to suffer their leading *him*. In practice he is prone to regard his own or the Institution's philosophy on an issue (and these are most of the time the same philosophies) as superior to any notions of his party.

163

When he calls on the party organization to assist him he is as likely as not to behave like the guest who not only lacks enthusiasm for the dinner being prepared but boldly goes out into the kitchen to take charge himself.

The manifestation of this typical Senatorial feeling may readily be seen at a national political convention. Senators usually hold high places in these proceedings, especially in regard to the platform committees, but they often have some visible difficulty in taking it all quite seriously. It is so disorderly, so noisy and so unattractive, as they see it, and the Senate's affairs are conducted, by comparison, almost as stately minuets with very little nonsense about the infallibility of majority rule.

XIII

THE SENATE

AND CRYPTO-INFLUENCES

THE STORY of overt political influences on the Senate and of
the Senate's counter influences in this field having been told,
it is well now to examine what might be called the play of

165

crypto-influences upon its members. Political instrumentalities and economic and other organizations have clearly defined motives in their dealings with the Senate. Other forces tending to some extent to shape its actions and decisions are in no sense organized and are far less consciously purposeful but nevertheless sometimes achieve results that are not inconsiderable.

These forces are basically non-political and for reasons of description they may be divided into the largely intellectual and the largely social. It is necessary, however, at once to subdivide the term "social" into what in this connection is important and what is not. What has significance here is the activity and attitudes common to the sentient society, that is, the thinking group, of Washington. Society with a capital S, the keepers of salons and the givers of parties, is not very relevant to the affairs of the Institution.

Though in some recent years it has been suspected of anti-intellectual bias, of hostility to intellectuals in general, the charge cannot be examined without inquiring into what kind of intellectualism is meant. It is true that the Senate has a prejudice against those intellectuals identified by strongly professorial conduct and views turned toward extreme innovations. It is also true, however, that intellectualism in its ultimate meaning, that is, a devotion to scholarly pursuits, is nowhere else in Government given so hospitable a welcome. And nowhere are purely rational arguments heard with greater respect. Here and here alone in Government

166

they need not be accompanied by mass support.

For a concrete illustration, the Executive Branch in the last analysis is first influenced by, and seeks first to influence, the common denominator of the press as represented by the news agencies. At the White House, in any administration, correspondents from the agencies are quite frankly given the better of it over the special writers. By long custom, an "agency man" asks the first question that sets off a Presidential press conference and he asks the one that brings it to a close. The newest of the mass mechanisms of communication, television, occupies so favored a place that it has wholly revolutionized proceedings.

In the Senate the contrast is great. To it the most influential political writers are almost never those with the greatest circulations, but are rather the truly intellectual journalists of Washington. In most domestic political affairs, the conservative Arthur Krock speaks with profound weight to the Institution—that is, to its dominant center—and his column is not syndicated. In foreign affairs, no voice is more persuasive than that of Walter Lippmann. Lippmann, like Krock, makes not the slightest attempt to converse with vast numbers, though his articles appear in many papers.

To all in the Institution who are slightly left of center the great man among the radio and television commentators is Elmer Davis. All three, Krock, Lippmann, Davis, significantly are elderly, long-established—and traditional. Equally significantly, they are highly individualistic men and anything but

167

typical, just as are the younger journalists who are moving up
in time to replace them—James Reston, the Alsop brothers,
Roscoe Drummond and others of their like.

There are many men in the Senate who would rather
have an approving reference by a Krock or a Lippmann than
a full laudatory column in the home town paper—except in
the extreme crisis time of a hard election year. For non-political influence operates in an untypical way in this place.
What is really valued there is the approval of the very influential few who it is assumed will in their turn and in due
course influenced the approval of the many.

There is little doubt, for an example, that not merely the
facts of international life and purely political pressures
caused the collapse of isolationism in the Senate as the Second World War drew to its close. At work here, too, was the
general *intellectual* climate of the Capitol, not at all measurable in terms of votes; the powerful, persistent hammering
of the most suitable parts of the press and the most suitable
of the scholars and pundits of all sorts. This hammering may
or may not at the start have been truly representative of the
general public feeling; more probably that feeling became
an effect and was never a cause.

For it often is the slow erosion of *attitudes*, rather than the
sharp thrust of demands, that moves the Senate, attitudes
that may be offered from the outside in an almost wholly
objective manner and without direct intention of influencing
the place. In this, by the way, may lie the reason for the odd

fact that television, whose unquestioning and unanalytical screen is the greatest boon that has yet befallen the general run of politicians, is still not really respected in the Senate. For television offers only one-dimensional exposition to the Senator who appears upon it; it has no ideas to put into interplay with his ideas. And then of course it should not be forgotten that television is new; the Senate recognizes its existence, of course, but suspects its *bona fides*.

Thus it is with *new* as distinguished from established professorial thought. Those who suppose the established kind of professorial thought to be unwelcome in the Senate should see the nodding of sagely approving heads when, say, the views on Constitutional law of old Professor Edward S. Corwin are invoked or when senior men from such a place as Cornell come forward with their papers on agriculture.

The purely social influences on the Senate are even more subtle and complicated than these others.

At any given time in Washington, hospitable women, for motives possibly having to do with lawful breaking and entering into the society pages, will be found to be operating large, glittering and competitive private salons. These have no public consequences visible to me, though I am far from expert in the matter, except possibly in the small sense that their occasional *nouveau riche* and rather small-town vulgarities may serve momentarily to amuse and thus to lighten the burdens of the politically adult.

Such soirees are, of course, attended by some of—but not

all—the members of the Senate. Candor, however, compels two highly unromantic observations. The first is that the motives of Senatorial guests often are no more complex than the simple desire for what is crudely called "free-loading." The other observation must wreck the cherished cliché vision of the glamorous hostess turning the course of a nation by the brilliance of her dinner-table conversation and the airy quality of her soufflés. There is, regrettably, nothing in all this at all.

Official entertainment, too, is rarely very influential, though this report, also, may run very much against folk myth. White House dinners, which somehow seem inescapably to have a strongly bureaucratic aftertaste, are not gladly attended by most Senators.

When the President and powerful members of the Institution wish, under social circumstance, to try their hand at influencing one or another they meet in a far less semi-public manner than this. There was, for example, a time when a good deal of high foreign policy was made in the Mayflower Hotel suite of Senator George, at which Secretary of State Dulles faithfully called at breakfast time once in a week when he was not engaged abroad.

Diplomatic parties are carefully "correct," and though relatively more popular than those given by the Executive Branch they necessarily have a certain feeling of arm's length which does not promote the free interchange of genuine opinion. These chiefly appeal to Senatorial wives who, alas, do not vote in the Institution and are, on the whole, not influential in that body except with the harassed housekeeping officials of the place like the Sergeant at Arms. (On a "big" Senate day this functionary must meet a series of crises in allotting the proper seats in the galleries to the "Senate ladies" and their guests.)

The kind of social pressure that has real effect on the Senate is the pressure of that which is the first meaning of the term *society*—a group of persons of common purpose or common interest. Of such groups, having a real if not a readily measurable influence upon the Senate, there are always several. Unlike the predominantly objective kind of intellectual influences already described these influences, though not wholly lacking in intellectual meaning, are primarily clique influences.

One group will be right wing in outlook; it was this group which, standing eagerly at the edge of the arena of real political action, so long and on the whole so vainly fought for the mind of the late Senator Taft. It sought to surround him socially with extreme nationalist writers, thinkers and propagandists, in every field from labor legislation to military and foreign policy. Another such group is left wing. It attempted for some two years almost physically to move in on Senator Humphrey of Minnesota who, it will be recalled, had come to the Senate as the great hope of the more advanced liberals. Humphrey and his wife Muriel, a down-to-earth blonde young woman with much steadying personal if not

171

political influence on her husband, at length in spirit showed these importunate visitors the door.

Then there is a centrist group whose social views, in the sense that the term is qualified here, have helped for years steadily to shape the dominant thought of the Institution. The easiest way to describe this group is to say that its notions and habits of life are such as to be of appeal at once to so thorough going a conservative as Byrd of Virginia and to so moderate a progressive as Senator John Kennedy of Massachusetts. It is made up primarily of writers, publicists, lawyers and other professional men.

The influence emanating from this body of persons—and even less than the two right and left bodies is it a consciously organized social force—is the greater for its restraint and the more enduring for its seemingly casual character. The Senate did not, for example, move against McCarthy until this social center had reached the unstated and informal but firm conclusion that this must be done.

The social center, which is always less precipitate and always less vehement than the left or the right, did not quickly or lightly reach the conclusion that McCarthyism had become a genuine national danger. Its ultimate feeling that this was so was all the stronger for its prior hesitation. But even then, as has been seen earlier, its influence was not enough to cause the Senate to attack McCarthyism itself but only to take limited action against McCarthy himself. All the same, it was a clear example of the partial success of an impalpable and non-partisan pressure upon the Institution.

This kind of pressure, which is an aura rather than a truly concrete thing, has, outwardly, the most gossamer quality and usually can be called social only in the fundamental meaning of that term.

Social pressures in the more common and snobbish meaning of the words are not, however, always absent and sometimes the Institution itself takes part in them. Consciously or not, and very curiously too, it responded to and in part condoned an almost wholly snob appeal in the case of President Truman. Mr. Truman, as has been said before, was never as a member of the Institution the truest of Senate types. Just so, he was not, when he was its presiding officer as Vice-President, looked up to quite as were such pro tem presidents of the Institution as Senators Vandenberg and, later, George.

Almost from the moment that Mr. Truman took the oath as President in succession to the dead Franklin Roosevelt a social pressure was arrayed against him, with a considerable degree of assistance from within the Senate, by the more emotional of the Roosevelt followers in and out of the Administration.

The consequence was the strange and still little-known or realized fact that the Truman Administration was actually from the start under sniping attack from the inside, alike from liberal Democrats who organizationally should have

173

welcomed and assisted him and from some conservative Democratic Senate types who simply did not hold him in high regard.

The element of snobbism entered in main part among the old New Dealers, whose understandable veneration of the memory of Mr. Roosevelt made them incapable of seeing anything good whatever in his accidental successor, Mr. Truman. These rather precious men simply could not forget that rather well-known Truman haberdashery. It is true that Mr. Truman himself did not help matters. He had an inborn and articulate distrust of and distaste for the Georgetown New Dealer—the pipe-smoking, tweed-jacketed martini-and-salad man who frequented this self-consciously tony and relatively Bohemian part of Washington while the Truman type of administrator went his unterrified way with his bourbon and cigar.

The fact is that long before there was general or sustained *Republican* attack on the Truman Administration many of the old New Dealers were, so to speak, opening the inner gates of the fortress and pointing out the soft spots to a partisan enemy not then even quite prepared to march. It should not be forgotten, either, that it was Senate committees controlled by the *Democrats* who prepared the way for much that followed in the ultimately successful general assault on Mr. Truman. Where but from these committees and others in the House arose the stories of the "five per centers," the mink coats, the deep freezes and all the rest?

174

Indeed, though it may not now be recalled, the most savage *initial* denunciation of his Administration came from liberal New Deal opinion-makers outside the Senate who as early as 1948 were in frantic search for an alternative to him at the Democratic National Convention and who in fact hotly courted the man they later found so altogether lacking, General Eisenhower.

Though incontestably there were other factors, a detached observer cannot rid himself of the conviction that the motive of this social pressure, where it arose outside the Senate, could not generally be disassociated from snobbery. Mr. Roosevelt was, perhaps, a great and matchless President and a war leader second only to Churchill. It is nevertheless a fact that to some in the Washington of his era and of the Truman era as well he was something other than this; his aristocracy as a person had to them an immense appeal and to many of his followers this was somehow a quality that they felt to be transferable to them.

At all events their form of social pressure helped open the way to the destruction of two decades of their own party's control of the White House. And to this a majority of the Institution consented to add to its own social pressure.

The principal meaning of this tale is this: The old New Dealers did not really know what they were about; they had no *wish* to open the field to their historic opposition. But the Senate knew quite well what *it* was about. On grounds that were far more objective, and certainly less unpleasant, this

175

essentially conservative body simply, and quite properly and logically from its point of view, did not care to have Mr. Truman remain as President—though unaccountably he refused to oblige this feeling. Clearly, Mr. Truman himself much preferred this kind of attitude to the other kind.

Thus, it may be seen that even the socio-intellectual pressures applied to the Institution may be turned about and adapted by it to its own ends.

But the old New Dealers mentioned here twice confused and compromised their loyalties and their interests. Their actions as disaffected partisan *Democrats* not only promoted the fortunes of the Republicans; their actions as then active or only recently resigned members of the Executive Branch weakened that branch in this one phase of its historic struggle for primacy with the Senate.

No part or wing of the Senate, however disenchanted for the moment with the rest of it, will *ever* apologize for the Institution itself, and certainly not in any power contest with the Executive. But some of the "good" Democrats of 1952—and the Executive Branch professional kind at that and not merely the justifiably more independent amateur Democrats—spent much of their time apologizing for their retiring President, Mr. Truman, and pulling their cloaks away from him and the other "bad" Democrats.

This course of moral hauteur was entirely permissible among the amateur Democrats and among all those *frankly* opposed to him. When, however, it was followed by professional Democrats with clear personal obligations to what was historically only a continuation of the Roosevelt Administration, it was to the wicked a wryly amusing spectacle.

Rarely had there been so desperate a search for respectability. The Institution itself, though beyond doubt respectable, is not all *that* respectable, and it smiled.

XIV

THE KERNEL

OF THE POWER

THE TRUE and ultimate power in the Senate resides in its standing committees, not in the kleig-lit, bellowing and transitory ones that chase alleged subversives or juvenile

179

delinquents but in the genuine old imperishable articles dealing day by day with the basic affairs of the United States.

It is here, often out of public view at the most decisive moments, that the real work is done and the whole drive of the place is most truly expressed. There are now fifteen standing committees of which two, those handling the business of the District of Columbia and the housekeeping administration of the Senate, are not especially relevant to great public issues.

Those actively and formidably engaged upon such issues are the Committees on Agriculture and Forestry, Appropriations, Armed Services, Banking and Currency (including the subject of economic controls, rationing and so on), Finance (tax raising), Government Operations (keeping a watch on what the Executive Departments of Government do and how they do it), Interior and Insular Affairs (supervising the Territories and so on), Interstate and Foreign Commerce, Judiciary, Labor and Public Welfare, Post Office and Civil Service, and Public Works.

A Senate committee is an imperious force; its chairman, unless he be a weak and irresolute man, is emperor. It makes in its field in ninety-nine cases out of a hundred the real decisions of the Institution itself. What bills it approves are approved by the Senate; what bills it rejects are rejected, with rare exceptions. There are far-separated times when a chairman loses his moral primacy over his issue or reaches with a majority of his committee a conclusion so starkly and hopelessly at variance with the wishes of the Senate generally that he is overruled.

But even then to repudiate his leadership and workmanship is a delicate and queasy task and one not relished by any general Senate majority, however great. If, reluctantly, it is undertaken, the victim is nearly always a *lesser* committee in the tradition of the Senate, say that on Labor. To override, say, the Committee on Foreign Relations or the Committee on Finance involves a parliamentary convulsion scarcely less severe, as the Senate sees it, than that accompanying the overturn, say, of a British government. And in fact the one crisis, a Senate decision overturning such a body as the Finance Committee, will hardly occur so frequently as will the other.

The Senate was comparatively slow in adopting the system of standing committees; it did not get around to this formally until the onset of the nineteenth century. But to what it had slowly embraced it soon began to cling with a fierce constancy. What it had rather leisurely established it found almost impossible, for any reason, to disestablish. Thus, a Committee on Revolutionary Claims, which was not set up until 1832, was not disbanded until 1921, surely a respectable distance in time from the war that had created these "claims."

At the start there was much backing and filling on the point as to how committee members ought to be selected, but by about 1830 custom had shaken down to the only method approved by reality. Selection became, as it has remained, the function of the party organizations in the Senate, the majority and minority leaders mutually agreeing on a full slate for each committee—with more places of course given to members of the majority party—and then obtaining the Senate's more or less routine concurrence. Today, there are differences, but they are more apparent than genuine, in the way the two parties go at the job. The Democratic slate for all committees is ostensibly prepared by the Democratic Steering Committee. The chairman of this Steering Committee, however, is the Democratic leader of the Senate, and it is he who in fact awards committee places, subject to other influences and circumstances.

A man of common sense, he will not, of course, go wholly and frontally against the wishes of the party patriarchs who surround him on the Steering Committee. He will attempt, too, so far as is possible, to give to each major section of the country (and thus to its vital interests) some kind of representation on each of the great committees. And he will attempt, also as far as is possible, to give each ideological section of his party a degree of recognition.

On the Republican side, a special Committee on Committees ostensibly makes the selections, subject to the endorsement of the organization of all the Republican members that is called the Conference. The chairman of the Conference, however (in recent years he was the imperturbable Millikin of Colorado), will appoint the Steering Committee. It need

182

not be supposed that he is overly restrained about suggesting what the Steering Committee, and then the Conference, ought to do. In doing so he will have regard to the wishes of the Republican Senate Leader, currently Knowland of California, and the chairman of the Republican Policy Committee, currently Bridges of New Hampshire.

Beyond all this, seniority, as to committee chairmanships, is an ineluctable and irresistible force. Chairmanships—thought this does not necessarily and always apply to those merely seeking committee membership—are not awarded by any party leader or group of hierarchs but, in nearly every instance, simply go to that man of the dominant party who has been longest on the committee. When a member comes to the Senate and is duly assigned to his committee he starts at the bottom and works up as death or defeat for re-election removes his seniors from the scene. There are more refinements: When two new committeemen are taken in on the same day one may be declared senior to the other simply because his State was the earlier of the two involved to enter the Union or even because the first letter of his name is found higher in the alphabet. Sometimes, in similar cases, seniority is decided by the toss of the coin.

Once a chairmanship is attained it is in practice not lost by any man so long as he remains in the Senate except on those occasions when his party loses control in an election and the other party for a time takes up the dominant role. The perquisite, therefore, with these qualifications may be considered to be for the political life of the holder; it is in this sense hardly less than an old-fashioned kingship.

For an extreme example of this peculiar vested interest there is the case of "Gumshoe Bill" Stone, who in 1917, when the United States was about to enter the First World War, was allowed by his Democratic colleagues to retain the chairmanship of the Foreign Relations Committee. Even though Stone, according to George H. Haynes in *The Senate of the United States,* was vindicated after a movement for his expulsion from the Institution on charge of treason, he was hardly the man to stand next to the President in making foreign policy.

Nevertheless, the illustration is an untypical one; for every Stone the seniority system has produced a score or more of able and learned committee chairmen. Much as the method has been deplored, it has never been put aside for two good reasons. The first is that the Senate would no more abandon it than it would abandon its name. The second is that at all events nobody has produced a really workable alternative.

Many reformers have cried out for choosing chairmen "only on ability." But who would decide "ability"? There is, moreover, the fact that nearly every committee chairmanship requires a literal expertness in the field involved—agriculture, taxes, foreign relations, and so on—and to acquire this sort of specialized lore there is no substitute for long experience.

There is the circumstance, too, that the Senate is basically the work and the home of old men; and old men are on the whole conservative men, for in a sense conservatism *is* age. Then, too, if a man's colleagues should simply ballot to determine, irrespective of his years of service, where he should sit, comparatively trivial factors certainly would intervene. Was Senator A more popular than Senator B? Would Texas and Arkansas line up together against Massachusetts and Rhode Island? And so on.

Reform in this field, as in a good many others, in short looks much easier the farther one stands from the facts.

As to the committee system generally, it neatly fits, as does so much else in the Senate, into the two-party system that has become a quasi-Constitutional part of American political life. It permits a clear division of power and responsibility between majority and minority. It sees to it that no minority *as between the two established parties* is transgressed. To splinter parties, however, it offers no *rights* but only sufferance, for these groups necessarily tend to distort if not to tear up the whole committee pattern.

The Populists and Free Silverites of a distant day put the Institution into turmoil, for it became hard to decide precisely at all times which of the major parties was at fault for what. The general history of the thing has been for the majority party, however grudgingly, to "take care" of splinter-party Senators.

And the phrase "to take care" of them has not usually had a benign meaning. The elder Senator Robert La Follette of

Wisconsin was frigidly treated, for organizational purposes, as a Republican, though he was in almost perpetual insurgence. He was given *certain* committee assignments by the Republicans, who had some understandable difficulty in regarding him as one of their own. But the one assignment he really wanted most he never got, not in twenty years of Senate service. What he had hoped for was membership on the Committee on Interstate Commerce. It has supervision over the railroads; and it was in handling railroad problems in Wisconsin that La Follette had become nationally known.

Again and much more recently, there was the affair of Senator Wayne Morse of Oregon. Morse entered the Senate in 1945 as a Republican, of a sort. He had not been there long before the orthodox in his party were casting at him glances of the utmost suspicion and by 1947 there was much Republican headshaking at his antics. He not only fought most of the Republican program in the Eightieth Congress; he grappled for its jugular vein in his opposition to the Taft-Hartley Labor Act. An able, courageous and contentious man of liberal views, he was day by day visibly less at home among his Republican colleagues. He made the tactical error, moreover, of applying early in his career for membership on the Foreign Relations Committee.

In the first place, he was junior and this request was a breach of Senate form, as it was understood by the Senate types in both parties. Older gentlemen were standing in line

186

already for that panoplied committee. In the second place, he was clearly not the favorite junior among the party elders, Taft in particular, so Morse kept missing the boat to the Foreign Relations Committee.

Undeterred, he persisted in being the thorn in the bush, the sand in the salad, to his presumptive brothers in the increasingly distrait Republican Senate fraternity. To this fraternity he had, so to speak, long since ceased to pay his dues, and its secret handclasps he had forgotten entirely, if indeed he ever knew them.

His cold war with the orthodox Republicans heated up tremendously in 1952; he broke off relations in an act of hot war and came out for the Democratic Presidential candidate, Adlai Stevenson. This the true Republicans regarded as nothing less than desertion in the face of the enemy; and Morse insisted on making it worse by openly ridiculing his detractors. As the Eighty-third Congress opened in 1953, with the Republicans newly in command there and General Eisenhower newly in the White House, there was an impasse in the Senate.

Morse, who had now become an Independent on the way to becoming a Democrat, declined to *ask* the Republicans to "take care" of him on committee assignments. Instead, he proclaimed the doctrine that he had an inherent *right* to retain his old committees, of which the principal one was Armed Services. The Republicans announced that since Senator Morse had declared himself no longer one of their

187

own he could have membership on—what? The very minor committees on the District of Columbia and Public Works. Morse now turned beseeching eyes upon the Democrats, but, somewhat uncomfortably, they looked the other way.

They declared, first, that it was the historic responsibility of the majority—in this case, the Republicans—to accommodate a splinter party—in this case made up of a membership of one. And, second, they insisted that to give really substantial Democratic committee seats to Morse would deprive members of the party faithful. And they argued, and history really would seem to support them, that for the Republicans to force the Democrats to take on an unwanted committeeman would breach the whole long chain by which things in the Institution are done more often by two-party consent than by rule. Still, they *did* hold out some hope to Morse. Come into the Democratic party, they told him in effect, and then we shall see.

This in fact he did and in 1954 he was instrumental in turning Senate control back to the Democrats, not only with his own vote but through his successful sponsorship of the first open Democrat to be elected to the Senate from Oregon in forty years, Richard Neuberger. All was now forgiven. In the Democratic Eighty-fourth Congress Morse not only got back on the Armed Services Committee, he climbed at last as well to the august bench of the Committee on Foreign Relations.

The reason was that *now* he was operating within the

framework of a committee system not only essential to the Senate but essential to a two-party system.

This saturnine prodigal son had dared the accumulated wrath of the whole Republican party in the Senate. What not even he could long continue to dare was the system within the system that makes the whole affair go forward as it does.

This system, like so much else in the Senate, is unique in government. The House of Representatives, of course, has standing committees, too; but with an enormous practical difference. Their chairmen, though far from powerless, nevertheless are subject to the sanctions and sometimes the bald and direct orders of the Speaker of the House and of its Committee on Rules, a body for which there is no Senate counterpart. The House Committee on Rules is a collective instrument of the leadership, that is, of the Speaker and his associates, and it takes up where the regular legislative committees have left off. They may clear a measure, but the Rules Committee can still keep it from the floor and thus cause it to remain inert.

In the Senate a committee chairman has no such parliamentary obstruction before him. True, he must look to the majority leader to schedule for floor action the business that he may bring from his committee. His designs thus can be slowed, but he remains their master all the same.

Even more important many times as a practical matter is his purely negative power. To approve any bill a committee must of course first meet; it meets only when its chairman says it shall. If on the docket there is a measure to which he is opposed and all his ordinary influence is not enough to halt it, he has yet another recourse. He can simply *not* call committee meetings until he has informal assurance that the particular matter to which he objects will not be brought up.

Hundreds and thousands of bills have been killed in this manner and while it may seem—and often is—a cavalier method, it is a noteworthy fact that the longer one observes the Institution the more inclined one is to suspect that inaction is frequently quite as good a thing or even a better thing than action. The Foreign Relations Committee, for illustration, has quietly put to sleep many an ill-timed, impetuous or sheerly demagogic proposal in foreign policy.

The varying chairmen have exercised this veto in their individualistic ways. It was the habit of Connally of Texas to make no secret of what he proposed to do, or rather not to do, with resolutions falling into one or another of these categories. Once, insistently pressed by the then very junior Senator Knowland to give a promise that he would act on a Knowland paper that the foreign-policy leaders all regarded as unwise, the Texan cried from the Senate floor in mock humility:

"I assure the Senator from California that his matter will have in the Foreign Relations Committee *exactly* the consideration that it so richly deserves." Here Connally looked up at the press galleries, grinned and passed his index finger across his throat like the blade of a knife.

Vandenberg as chairman of the Foreign Relations Committee was more bland in manner when he intended to put the fatal chill on some enterprise referred to that committee. He simply found himself too busy to put that particular question to a vote. George, still later on, had a third tactic. At proposals he might regard as hopelessly unsuitable he would stare in the committee with a kind of weary and incredulous distaste, simply refusing to recognize them at all. It is said that in ordinary life one cannot rid himself of unpleasant things simply by willing them to go away; but a powerful Senate committee chairman very often can do just that.

Any session of the Senate in any Congress will show that this is so, just as it will show that the chairman of a single committee often can speak with all the practical authority of the ninety-six members of the whole Senate. In the Eighty-fourth Congress, Byrd, as chairman of Finance, over and over did exactly that. He had no difficulty in informing the Secretary of State what the Administration could and could not have in regard to tariff authority; a brisk Byrd sentence told the Secretary of the Treasury what he could and could not have in the way of debt-limit and tax legislation.

Similarly, a chairman of the Senate Judiciary Committee, the late Kilgore of West Virginia, informed what presumably must have been a majority of the Senate itself, since a majority had initially backed the enterprise, that there would be no Bricker amendment to limit the Presidential treaty power in the first session of the Eighty-fourth Congress. Kilgore simply did not allow the Judiciary Committee to act on a proposal already once rejected by the Senate itself. If many members of the Senate were resentful or even regretful they masked their feelings. It is more likely that many were relieved to be able to avoid a final decision on a thing that looked a bit less attractive to them as time went on.

But while the general power of negation specifically exercised here by a Kilgore as chairman of Judiciary was pleasing alike to the Eisenhower Administration, to internationalists in general and most liberals in particular, its very existence was shortly to distress much the same groups.

Kilgore's death in 1956 opened the chairmanship, by a rule of seniority that in more than a century and a half has only three times been set aside by the Senate, to Senator James Eastland of Mississippi. Eastland was widely known as a bitter and vehement racist, and he had denounced the Supreme Court for its decision outlawing racial segregation in the public schools as a high bench that had been "indoctrinated and brainwashed by left-wing pressure groups."

Here was, for the Institution itself and even more for the controlling Democrats, a great dilemma. The whole long history of the place automatically gave the chairmanship to Eastland as the senior surviving Democratic member. But this was a committee holding primary jurisdiction over nearly all forms of civil-rights legislation (Eastland as a chairman of a subcommittee on the matter had once omitted to hold a single meeting in two years). It was, moreover, a committee with supervisory powers over the whole of the Federal judiciary, not excluding the Supreme Court, of which he had spoken in such extraordinary and shocking terms.

If the Democratic party as a party had been able to have its way Eastland's accession would never have been allowed, for all those deeply interested in civil rights felt that his elevation to a place of ultimate power over these matters was simply intolerable. The Senate, however, remained the Senate. It rather glumly but manfully promoted Eastland to the chair on unanimous motion of a Senate Democratic Steering Committee that closed ranks, as nearly always they are closed when the Institution must meet pressure from "the outside."

Two Senators and two alone arose in protest—Morse of Oregon and Lehman of New York as leaders of the liberal bloc. And even they were measured and careful in their strictures; they spoke impersonally of Eastland and they made no effort to depreciate the strength of the long custom that was here on trial.

What the incident has done and will do to the Democratic party is one story; long before the 1956 elections Eastland had been adopted as a symbol of reaction by many and the Republicans had found great use in the issue in the Negro voting wards and in others. For the Senate, however, the greater duty—greater, indeed, than all the complex of issues symbolized by Eastland—lay in the preservation of its traditions of place and power.

For, again, this power, whether in the chairman of the Appropriations Committee, the Armed Services Committee, or another, is legendary. A Judiciary Committee chairman can force (and often has forced) an administration toward its knees by refusing to act, as the first necessary step in Senate confirmation, on its appointments to the judiciary. (Langer of North Dakota as Judiciary chairman in the Eighty-third Republican Congress allowed an investigation to be made of Chief Justice Earl Warren in such hostile, police-court terms as to enrage the Republican Senate leader, Knowland. Knowland seemed to be threatening reprisals at one point; old Langer, secure in one of the most secure of Senate traditions, publicly dared his detractors to try to remove him as chairman. Nobody tried.)

An Appropriations Committee chairman can literally strike terror into the hearts of the bureaucrats, for he can go a long way toward withholding the money necessary for operations. From this great post chairmen have endlessly harassed those officials and activities that were not to their taste.

From this same place Bridges of New Hampshire, who no doubt honestly believed and continued to believe that the Eisenhower Administration was not sufficiently aware of some aspects of the Communist threat, in 1953 sent to a reluctant State Department one of its least-welcomed recruits, Scott McLeod, as its security officer. Again and again the Appropriations Committee—and most of the time this phrase is a

194

mere euphemism for the simple word "chairman"—has altered or reversed high administration designs.

All this is true in some degree of every one of the thirteen great Senate standing committees; no man and no force, not even a popular President, will lightly or wisely cross them if there is an alternative. This, again, illustrates one of the senses in which the place is a great deal more than merely a lawmaking body.

In this essential function, that is, lawmaking, that which is clearly good in the committee system well outweighs all that is bad to very bad. The roster of any Senate committee will be found to represent a vast continuity of many years of understanding in a particular field. It must be recalled that men in the Executive Department often are mere novices; when Charles Wilson came from General Motors to the Pentagon in 1953 not even his closest friends could have argued that he knew his new terrain. But on the Senate Armed Services Committee were men who had been dealing with the Pentagon and its predecessor organizations since long before the Second World War. Its chairman in the Eighty-fourth Congress, Russell of Georgia, had been a powerful and informed member years before either Wilson himself or a single one of his chief current military advisers had held any significant place in the top military establishment of the United States.

And this was so of many of Russell's colleagues, one of the more junior of whom, by the way, Symington of

195

Missouri, had served as Secretary of the Air Force.

The general facts are alike with respect to any Senate committee in the area of its jurisdiction. Thus, the preparation of an important bill begins in what are objectively good auspices; it is to be handled by men who know the subject and who, by and large, have a special fondness for it. They will be assisted, moreover, by professional staffs of high skill; these, in my observation, are as a group rarely matched for ability and devotion to duty.

The hearing itself will take a familiar course. Those for the bill will be invited in, and then those against it. Examination and cross-examinattion will of course vary, committee by committee, in terms of essential aptness and degree of disinterested inquiry. Generally speaking, however, these affairs are truly fruitful in the best sense of the word. In such matters the Institution expects that every man will do his duty, for the ultimate decision of the Senate itself will most of the time really be drawn up in this committee room. It may be the small, rococo, gilded room of the Foreign Relations Committee, set grandly in the Capitol itself, or one of the large, echoing chambers used for committee work in the Senate Office Building. Wherever the scene, the basic work is nearly always the same. Nearly always there is a long, leisurely exploration of every possible facet of the matter at hand; for if anybody is in a hurry he will simply swallow his impatience. Questioning from the committee bench proceeds in the immemorial way—by seniority—first from the top man on the majority side, then to the top man on the minority side, back again to the majority side, and so on.

The record being made here will at length be carried to the floor of the Institution itself; and on almost every occasion it is a complete and a careful record.

At length, as the time comes for the committee's decisions, the room will be cleared of all save Senators and, sometimes, their staff assistants. The chairman will put the questions: Shall the bill be amended, then shall it be reported favorably, or, in the old-fashioned phraseology, with the recommendation "that it do pass"?

All is quiet, all is casual; men having oratory in mind will save *that* for the Senate floor. Again, as in so many of its critical moments, it is *smallness* that characterizes the Institution: a handful of quiet, intent men in a room now shut away from all turmoil in making a decision. Perhaps it is simply to add peanuts to the subsidized farm commodities. But perhaps it is to take the United States of America to war. Whichever it may be the point of action arrives casually and with a quiet, deliberate gravity. The committee report is prepared, perhaps with a minority report in dissent, and the job is done.

XV

THE HUMAN

DIFFERENCES

To SAY, as has so often been said in this book, that the Senate has oneness is not to diminish or blur the great human dividing line that follows the straight course of the center aisle which sets off the parties from one another. Most men here are alike in the deep sense that they are Senate men, joined in a common pride in the meaning and traditions of their forum. To outside attack from any source, not excluding the White House, they will certainly turn a common face, and they are at the end members of the Senate even before they are members of political parties.

Humanly, however, there are sharp variations between the common run of the Democrats who sit here and the common run of the Republicans. These are differences quite beyond the limited number of genuinely fundamental differences in ideology between the two parties. It is hardly too much to say that they are differences between two kinds of people.

For there is not only a Senate type; there is then a Senate-Republican type and a Senate-Democrat type. The distinguishing marks of each may be said, parenthetically, to distinguish the parties in a more general sense. What is here attempted, however, is only to suggest how these divergencies are visible in the Institution, what their effects may be, and how they may possibly bear upon the future.

A young lady of my acquaintance once said of the Republican Senate leader, Knowland of California, when asked to characterize him after a first meeting: "He just *looks* like a Republican." The comment was intuitively correct even if it was wholly subjective. For there *is*, in a sense, a Republican *look* and a Democratic *look*, if the term is used to suggest

the sum total of the appearance, the personality, the habits
and the activities of the one partisan and the other.

In making every effort to avoid the merely fanciful, it must
be conceded at once that the Republican side of the aisle
in a given session of the Senate could not in the human
sense be said exactly and totally to characterize the same
side of the aisle in any and every other session. And the
same, of course, goes for the Democratic side. It is possible,
nevertheless, generally to characterize either side of the
aisle in any session known to this writer.

The Republican side will be found to have these small
common factors: There is an almost touchable sense of
decorum and discipline, a circumstance likely to make the
task of any Republican leader rather less difficult than that
of any Democratic leader. There is a habit of punctuality
and order, so that Republican members as a group are less
laggard in appearing when the noon bell opens proceedings
and less likely to stray away at odd moments. There is a
far more nearly fixed routine in operations. Of the current
leaders Knowland will almost always be found planted
solidly, determinedly and carefully in his proper chair, putting his attention punctiliously ahead on the presiding
officer. Johnson of Texas, for the Democrats, is either to be
seen lounging on the base of his spine in his seat, whispering
loudly and cheerfully to his colleagues around him, or,
more likely, not in his seat at all but roaming restlessly about
and sometimes—before his heart attack in 1955—cupping

an illicit cigarette in his hand near the last back exit to the chamber.

The common Republican mien is both businesslike and faintly solemn. The common Democratic mien is casual, gossipy, relaxed and highly prone to private jokes, un-parliamentary laughter, tardiness, absenteeism except when the chips are down, and a certain spirit hospitable to minor hell-raising in general. Democratic Senators know their seat-mates intimately; Republican Senators know their seatmates well.

In a great debate, the Republican participants will usu-ally, often with mounds of their homework on their desks before them, be visibly prepared. The Democrats, as they rise one by one on their side, are as a class more inclined to proceed ad lib, sparring jocularly as they do so with their party colleagues as well as with the Republican opposition and gladly seizing upon interruptions from any quarter in the hope, wistful or otherwise, that from most any source may come unexpected assistance. The Republicans generally are a bit more untrustful when colloquies begin; in their basic inclination to suspect hostile intent from a Democratic interrogator they often are right but often quite unneces-sarily alarmed.

The essential thread of debate is in consequence usually more faithfully and more coherently followed from the Re-publican side. To hear three major speeches from that side on a great issue is to grasp quite clearly what is the essential

Republican position. The Democrats, however, are not good at following any thread.

In every sense less orderly than their Republican opponents, they may follow each other as speakers in whatever sequence chance may indicate, and they may not at this point even in the vaguest sense appear to follow each other's reasoning. When the final test comes, however, it is as likely as not that the inchoate nature of the general Democratic presentation may be suddenly transformed into an almost monolithic voting record. It will simultaneously be plain, in retrospect, that these many and seemingly totally different aspects of the Democratic case have formed a mosaic in which each part of the debate has its fitting place. It will be found that the planless had a certain plan, after all.

The sum of the Republican argument, in the meantime, will at the end be seen as about what it was at the very beginning. The Republican case will not have been so much broadened and expanded as fortified and refortified.

It is fair, therefore, to say that the level of Democratic debate, as debate, is nearly always the higher, as its form is nearly invariably the more graceful, whether or not Democratic objectives may be more or less elevated in a particular case. Exposition, tireless, dogmatic, stubborn, repetitive and clear, is the Republican method. Humor, satire, suggestion, a greater and readier degree of eloquence, a swooping, circular approach to the objective—this is the Democratic method.

The Republican singleness of purpose is not consciously avoided by the Democrats; it is simply that they are for the most part temperamentally incapable of it except on the very rare occasions when their leaders are able to cajole and corner them into something resembling a unified approach in debate. Like all improvisers, they are not inclined to keep a line long even when it is good. The Republicans for their part, more prudent and more frugal in the intellectual sense, are not the men to abandon a useful technique or issue simply because it is well worn. I recall, for illustration, an occasion when half a dozen or so Democrats, more for the sport of it than for anything else, were pressing the Republicans on some aspect or another of their ordinary domestic policies. Knowland, the Republican leader, rose and, belligerently facing the Democrats, solemnly demanded of them: And what about Alger Hiss?

The question, in the partisan political sense, was perfectly legitimate, for a Democratic Administration clearly had responsibility for Hiss as one of its officials. It arose, however, so far out of the context of the moment (context is the only word for there is no rule requiring relevancy in Senate debates) as simply to leave the laughing Democrats incredulous.

These contrasts in debate between the men of the two parties in the Institution spring, of course, from even more personal contrasts. While nothing here is truly "average" it might be said that the representative Republican has in truly personal relationships, precisely as in debate, a less skillful personal touch than the representative Democrat. He is not, in a word, the man whom a fellow smoker in the club car would quickly approach to strike up an idle conversation. It is not that he is unfriendly or formidable; he simply is not quite so readily likable as is his Democratic vis-à-vis.

Young employees around the Institution sometimes will use affectionately disrespectful words about its Democratic members. One, a young member notably gallant with the ladies, has sometimes been called "the Shoreham Flash," in reference to that hotel's locally well-known facilities for dining and dancing and wining. I have even heard the Jovian George, in all the dignity of his great place and years, referred to by Senate employees as "the Brain." I never heard them call a Republican Senator anything other than Senator So-and-So.

Again the representative Republican member is far less gregarious and convivial than his Democratic opposite number. Not to put too fine a point on it, the Democrats run more often to fairly bibulous types, just as—determinedly non-conformist though they are—they have more absolute teetotalers.

These matters are not mere trivia, though at first glance they might seem to be. Together, they tell a human story of some importance, for the small and incidental as well as the large and purposeful have real effects in politics. They might even indicate why the Democratic side of the Senate tends on the whole to be less responsible in the purely fiscal sense and more compassionate in the purely human sense.

Certainly, they *accompany*, whether or not they inherently influence, one of the profound facts of life in the Senate. This fact, which is significant to every person concerned in public policy, is observable, one believes, to every close attendant on the Institution, whatever his political feeling. It is that the Republican party, in the Senate at least, is suffering from a serious relative shortage in professional political talent relative to that available to the Democrats.

This observation has nothing whatever to do with questions as to which party is *right* about this or that issue; it concerns which party is more *effective* on this or that issue. The simple answer is that the Democrats (perhaps in part because the Senate is so eminently suited to the long-lived Southerners) are far the more able party politically, in their front-line personnel and also in their reserves.

In the Senate of the Eighty-fourth Congress, when the party division was forty-nine Democrats to forty-seven Republicans, a detached analysis would show twenty-one Republicans of fair to good proved or clearly prospective technical ability as against at least thirty-three in these categories among the Democrats. Political *attitudes* are in no way involved here; this list runs from such a man as Case

206

of New Jersey to such a man as Dirksen of Illinois.

The disparity as to the younger members of the Institution, those upon whom in future most will depend, was even greater. Twenty-four Democrats in this age category could fairly be said to be technically and professionally valuable, in fact or in reasonable promise, against twelve Republicans. Again, the lists of the valuable in both parties in this bracket run in political orientations from the left to the extreme right.

The point makes itself that this state of affairs, in which the common ability of one party in the Senate is visibly higher than that of the other—quite apart from mere numerical considerations—is not a good one. Among the most curious of the related phenomena is that, at least from 1946 onward, each successive infusion of "new" Republican blood cannot possibly be objectively and generally described as of service to that side of the aisle. The very reverse is in general unhappily true.

What has often been called in the Senate "The Class of Forty-six," meaning the group of Republican members first elected in that year, included such members as Senators McCarthy of Wisconsin, Jenner of Indiana, and Malone of Nevada. None is a true Senate type; none can be said, in all honesty, to have contributed usefully to the traditions either of the Institution or his own party. And oddly not one of the three—of whom McCarthy was actually the most nearly moderate in *general* political view—can be said to have been of much lasting intellectual service to the far-right wing to which all have been in varying degrees devoted.

The fact is that this far-right wing, which has a perfectly valid place in the affairs of the Institution, must in the nature of the case depend primarily on voices within the Republican side for its adequate—and, needed—presentation. And those who are really capable of articulating its policies are men like Knowland of California and Bridges of New Hampshire, who are capable of doing so only on certain issues and at certain times. They are not, that is to say, really and totally right wingers, though they have been put into that category by the oversimplifications of many political writers.

It is true that the Democratic side of the Institution suffers something of a kindred disability, to a lesser extent, in the fact that its left wing has been shrunken, in influence if not in numbers, in about the same period. The Democratic left wing, nevertheless, has remained relatively much more coherently articulate than has the Republican right—and largely for purely human and personal and institutional reasons. The center, as has heretofore been pointed out, is historically dominant, in both parties.

It is, however, humanly impossible for the Democratic center to press so implacably, and thus so effectively, upon the dissident fringes on its side of the aisle as does the Republican center.

208

This circumstance no doubt is a factor in creating the basic point—the higher degree of general Democratic ability in the purely practical and forensic sense. At any rate, the parties, however nearly matched they may be in numbers, are not closely matched in the skills of the place, as could be seen time and again in the Eighty-fourth Congress.

Expressed in practical terms, the result was this: Johnson for the Democrats in any parliamentary crisis, large or small, could call upon a far larger number of capable stars and reserves, whether the need of the moment was in the field of debate or in the field of "operating," than could Knowland for the Republicans. "Operating," indeed, is one of the particular strong human points of the Democrats in the Senate. The term is very loose and flexible but it involves such human activities as these: the art of informal persuasion, the instinctive grasp of what is the more nearly useful thing to attempt in an emergency, the sensory understanding of the weaker places in the phalanx drawn up by the opposition in any given context of circumstances.

Johnson, himself, for an example, or any one of his principal deputies, usually could sense quite as quickly as could Knowland, with his far closer contact with the Administration Republicans, on what ground the Administration was likely to settle in the end on any issue before the Senate.

This did not, of course, for a moment mean that Johnson was a *superior* man to Knowland; it only meant that he was

209

a more intuitive man, operating with more freedom of motion in a more relaxed party. To put it another way, the stiffness of Knowland, an honorable and very downright man quite incapable of subtlety, had a kind of inevitability in the very human nature of his party. The flexible, inventive, more volatile characteristics of Johnson were in a sense really the human characteristics of *his* party. The Republican side of the Institution will make its high plans and lock them away, so to speak, unalterable in the deepest vaults. The Democratic side is more likely to write its operational secrets on an old envelope and then toss it on top of the bureau among the litter.

The Republican Senate Policy Committee will meet once a week, but it will do so only upon carefully printed notices circulated to the committee's members officially to inform them that there *is* to be a meeting. The Democratic Policy Committee will meet—perhaps—once a week, and when it does the thing seems simply to happen and members will stroll in, usually late, with the air of a man dropping into another's office to have a drink and, having nothing better to do at the moment, to pass the time of day.

Again, any member of the Democratic Policy Committee, assembled over a topic however grave, will when the spirit moves him inquire even of its clerks and staff people for their opinions on such and such. There was in 1955 an occasion when the question for discussion was what attitude the Democrats should take toward the crisis involving the offshore islands and Formosa. Bobby Baker, the twenty-seven-year-old secretary of the Democratic majority's organization, earnestly observed to the seventy-seven-year-old Senator George when called upon: "Senator, I can tell you this: I for one haven't lost a single damn thing on Quemoy or Matsu."

Imagination boggles at attempting to conceive any such scene, or any such words from employees, in the Republican Policy Committee. Imagination simply will not try the jump.

XVI

WHY NOT VERY MANY SENATORS BECOME PRESIDENT

ONE OF the best ways for an elevated public man *not* to become President—using a little exaggeration for emphasis —is to serve in the Senate of the United States. In all its

213

long history this greatest of American political institutions has sent only thirteen of its members to the Presidency. (If one were dealing in any other equation of political posts this, no doubt, would seem a high enough percentage. But it ought to be borne in mind that while the United States has had thirty-three Presidents it has had some three thousand Senators.) Of these thirteen, only three—Monroe, Andy Jackson and Truman—can be said to have added in the White House to the luster of their careers. And at least one, Mr. Truman, never ceased even in the finest hours of his executive life to long with one part of his spirit for the old place that he had left.

Not one of the Senate's most distinguished members has reached the White House at all. A single year, 1952, saw the denial of Presidential nominations to two of the Senate's finest, Senator Richard B. Russell of Georgia by the Democrats and Senator Robert A. Taft of Ohio by the Republicans. Four years earlier, in 1948, a third, Senator Arthur H. Vandenberg of Michigan, was not so much rejected outright as shunted aside, with his own unspoken consent. He failed of the nomination primarily *because* he was a Senate man; because he had since 1946 been throwing himself so passionately into the largely selfless work that characterizes the Senate at its best. He had, in his one-man campaign to draw the Republican party toward his own newly adopted internationalism without wrecking it in the process, become too *reasonable* to head a purely partisan national campaign

214

against the Democrats. He fell victim as an embodiment of one of the Institution's most changeless drives, its drive toward accommodation and compromise.

An ex-isolationist, he was not forgiven by the isolationist group still then powerful within his party. A late-comer to the newly dominant policy of interventionism, he typified the party's new search for the great verities in world life. But he had reached this point in his thinking in the poky, old-fashioned, inconsistent way that the Senate regards as illustrating the proper growth of wisdom but which the non-institutional people regard as illustrating only the regrettable quality of hem and haw in this place. Knowing he likely could not be nominated he did not really try.

In 1952, Russell, though he made a hard run for it, never approached success for more complicated reasons. Being a Senate type was not in this instance the primary reason, though it would have been quite enough in any case. For Russell had first of all to combat the powerful, intractable fact that he was a Southerner. If it is true, as has been observed earlier, that the Senate is for the South a place to exact recurring counter-reparations for the War Between the States, it is equally true that the Presidency is a place for the exaction of an unending Northern revenge. While it is a fact that Southern memories and resentments of the old conflict are, politically and otherwise, far more active than those of the North (and can become quite tiresome), it is equally a fact that subconsciously at least the North for nearly a century has put an impenetrable bar against the elevation of *any* real Southerner to the White House.

Those aspirants who tend to have Southern sympathies will be well advised to keep them hidden. (There *have*, by the way, been such men; and quite recently. Mr. Truman, of all people, civil rights and all, and for all of the fact that so much of the South so disliked him, had all during his career a touch of split personality in connection with this subject. His intellectual convictions, and his political necessities, required him to make his strongest alliance with Northern Democrats. There is little question in my mind, however, that in his heart he really *preferred*, as men, the Southern Democrats—all of them, that is, who were not seeking his destruction. He had, for example, no closer friend than Sam Rayburn of Texas, the Speaker of the House of Representatives. In the gloomy day in the spring of 1945 on which Franklin Roosevelt died and Mr. Truman became President he received the news in the Capitol office of Rayburn. On the fifth anniversary of that event, President Truman came back to Rayburn's office, on his own request, to commemorate that day in history.

(Again, Adlai Stevenson of Illinois has a great deal more of the South in him, made up though it is of impalpables and imponderables, than the country at large ever supposes. He was, in 1952 and in 1956, in fact, in many basic matters a good deal closer to the philosophy of the Southern leader Russell than to such a Northern leader, say, as Lehman of New York.)

And, wholly apart from the irreparable disability simply of being a Southerner, Russell never in any likely event would have been accepted by the 1952 Democratic convention. He had the common Senatorial characteristic of being alien, in the last, deep analysis, to the whole concept necessarily underlying either a Presidential convention or a Presidential campaign, the concept of unqualified majority rule. At Chicago that year he persisted in the techniques and in the fundamental views of the Institution itself because he *knew* no others. His techniques, in a word, were suitable to the relatively quiet chamber of the Senate but wholly inadequate to catch and convince the passing crowd. His views still sought the line of the careful center in the last place on earth where that line is real and tenable, a sweating convention hall where power is the first and last answer and where power arises from passion and prospect of victory.

And it was largely so with Taft among the Republicans in 1952, as indeed it had been with him in 1948. Here was a man who by any objective reckoning was incomparably the outstanding *Republican* in the United States—in either year—right or wrong though he may have been in his policies. He was, however, operating in what for him was simply the wrong forum, as was his friend Russell, as would have been Vandenberg in 1948 had he pressed his claims, and similarly with Webster two lifetimes before.

For the Institution is hardly the place for the training necessary either to seize a Presidential nomination or, having seized it, to turn it into election at the polls. It has become a severe, unwritten law of politics in recent years that being Senatorial all but disqualifies a man to be Presidential. And where this rule has been broken the consequences on the whole have not been happy. For every ex-Senator who has become a striking President, significant in the positive sense to his age and time, there have been two or more ranging from the positively bad to the drearily futile or mediocre or simply sad. For one Truman, there has been a Van Buren, a Benjamin Harrison or a Harding. For one Andy Jackson there has been a Tyler, a Pierce or a Buchanan. For one Monroe there has been a William Harrison, an Andrew Johnson.

Some have taken the view that, in modern times at any rate, the strong national resistance to any Senatorial nominee for the Presidency arises from the malodor and the intellectual squalor of the Administration of the tragic Harding.

The explanation seems wholly insufficient; just as the unfortunate Administration of General Grant did not, for example, rule out the nomination and the considerable success of General Eisenhower's Administration, though this latter general, too, was both a war hero and a professional military man.

A good case could be made that this resistance is far deeper and far more soundly based, in national instinct if not in national consciousness. For the qualities that make a good Senator are in no important way those that make a good President. The Presidency, it cannot be emphasized too much in this connection, is an *administrative* function, by necessity perpetually modern and current in outlook. The Institution is basically a philosophical function, by necessity comparatively antique and historical in outlook. The most generally successful and venerated Presidents of this country have been men not only unafraid of innovations but positively welcoming them.

Theodore Roosevelt shook up the Republican party, in its traditions and purposes, as no man has ever done since Lincoln, who could not really shake up what he himself founded.

Woodrow Wilson took the incredible risks not only of creating the New Freedom as precursor to the New Deal; upon that section of his party that is pro-Executive rather than pro-Senate he implanted a faintly professorial cast that has survived to this day. Franklin Roosevelt, it goes without saying, revolutionized his party, outside the Senate, as well as the country.

And it is an arresting fact that no Presidents in history— with the possible exception of Mr. Truman, who also was an innovator as an uncharacteristic Senate man—were more implacably fought by the Institution than were these three. It was not simply that they had ideas and policies that evoked much basic antagonism in the Senate. Almost equally important was the simple fact that they were insisting upon taking strange new roads calculated to lead to very doubtful places.

As one observer, I take it that the era of Theodore Roosevelt was good for the country and for the promotion of the Presidency. It was, however, not good so far as the Institution saw it then—and really sees it now. For while Theodore Roosevelt, at least for a time, brought the Republican party up to date with facts of national political life, he created for the *Senate* wing of that party something sharper than the old inherent sense of alienation between the Senate and the Executive power.

The lasting quality of this heightened alienation was easily observable even in the first year of the Eisenhower Administration; the Senate wing of the party never in full free will followed him, not even at the flood tide of his power and influence. He was, however moderate he saw his own role, quite too devoted to the present and the future at the expense of the past.

Again the story of Woodrow Wilson's relationship with the Senate is not to be dismissed simply as an example of the pointless vexations visited upon a good and imaginative man by an old and sterile forum, the Senate. Wilson, so profoundly Presidential was he, was thereby *necessarily* un-Senatorial. In undertaking almost alone to bring about the extraordinary device called the League of Nations, he reckoned without the Senate, which broke his great dreams and brought them down into embittered ruin.

The point of the moment is not whether Wilson was justified in what he did; Constitutionally he was. The point is only that this Tennysonian concept (". . . the Parliament of Man, the Federation of the world") was typically Presidential, and almost *atypically* Senatorial. As an Institution it has not yet, in fact, gladly confirmed the concept even of national sovereignty over the States.

It accepted, in the later United Nations, a limited concept of world sovereignty but only because this was accompanied by a big-power veto that was, of course, more a reaffirmation than a surrender of national sovereignty.

And the Franklin Roosevelt era, good and wise nationally though in many ways it may have been, was accompanied by Presidential attitudes and acts some of which were simply inconceivable to the Senate. What, for illustration, was that place to make of a President who publicly urged the adoption of a bill regardless of the admittedly strong presumptive Constitutional objections to it?

Or of a President whose program unquestionably increased the small man's *economic* freedom before the law but whose influence seems rather clearly to have been followed by an attitude in the Supreme Court in which *any* man's truly *inti-*

mate freedom often seems less defended? (It may be curious but is historically a fact that the old "reactionary" court, precisely when it was tossing out economic sanctions intended to aid the needy, was stopping the Government in it tracks every time it sought to establish any aspect of a "loyalty oath." The new "liberal" court, on the other hand, has been able to deal softly with the extraordinary argument that even the court itself cannot be trusted with certain of the "secret" data gathered by the security officers.)

Nevertheless, there is no purpose here to add to the endless disputations concerning the three strongest Presidents of our generation. The purpose is only to show why Senators so rarely become Presidents and why it is that they are ill-fitted to the Presidency anyhow. The habit of mind and action of the Senate almost certainly could not have halted the Depression in time. Almost certainly it could not have coped with Hitler and his accomplices until coping was too late.

It is, however, only this habit of mind and action that has on the whole steadily kept alive certain traditions that may be nearly as important as defeating the Depression and not infinitely less important than winning the war.

The Senate's habit of mind and action, indeed, is almost by definition not the habit of mind and action of any strong Executive. It is, moreover, primarily in times dominated by aggressive Executives that the Senate attempts most vigorously to enter into truly national and truly partisan politics.

It is said by wise and experienced political writers that one of the very rare instances where Senators rather than other political functionaries have ultimately controlled a political convention was on the occasion of the nomination of Harding by what is sometimes called a "Senate regency." Without disputing this point it is a fact that this was a very atypical incident; and a fairly good argument could be made, moreover, that what occurred here was not so much the emergence of a Senate clique of power as an erratic abdication of the ordinary political power. Harding was in no sense distinguished in the Institution from which he so unaccountably came forward to the Presidency.

Generally it has been the case (a) that the Senate deeply intervenes in political conventions only against *strong* Presidents and (b) that almost always it fails therein. It is extremely doubtful that even a majority of the Senate Democrats truly welcomed the third nomination of Franklin D. Roosevelt. It is an undoubted fact that Democrats in the Institution provided, *sub rosa* or otherwise, much of the intellectual opposition.

And there is no question at all that the general weight of the Senate was against Mr. Truman's nomination in his own right in 1948 after he had served a part of a term in succession to Franklin Roosevelt. While the right-wing Democrats were more openly in the van against him—as for illustration the extreme exertions of Byrd of Virginia to find a way to sidetrack the Truman candidacy at the convention—there was almost *no* really favorable Democratic feeling to him in all the Institution.

Mr. Truman, like another ex-Senator before him who became President, Andy Jackson, was to the Senate the genuine apostate: He had been a *member* and yet here he was, knocking the Institution about as though it had no overweening significance in the scheme of things.

The central truth is that the Executive Department and the Senate have no genuine *understanding* of each other, in the sense that understanding means sympathetic perception and tolerant comprehension.

In the years that this writer has observed the scene in Washington at rather close hand he has never known an important occasion when the White House really and deeply understood the Senate or when the Senate actually and deeply understood the White House. This circumstance cannot possibly be due only to the ordinary clashes of personalities and parties and political ideologies, for a Democratically controlled Senate understood Mr. Truman no better in any important sense than one in Republican hands and vice versa. The same was true through the first years of the Eisenhower Administration.

There is between the two seats of power something of a deep divergence that does not lie between any other two seats of power—not, for example, between the White House and the House of Representatives or between the White

House and the Supreme Court. The one, the Senate, is basically unreconstructed from the very old days; the other, the White House, is at any moment an illustration of what is good and strong in *current* American life and what may be bad, or simply in bad taste.

XVII

SENATE INVESTIGATIONS,

MIXED

The most controversial and least clearly defined of all the powers of the Senate, the power to conduct investigations, has many times in history far overshadowed the Senate's basic functions. The mere words "Senate investigation" bring up visions of leaping headlines—and more recently of clattering radio and television sets. There is the memory of the dark brow and the mechanical monotone of Senator McCarthy (*"Mr. Chairman: Point of Order!"*) as some thirty years before there was the compelling image of Senator Walsh of Montana and his associates as they explored the labyrinths of the Harding Administration.

Whatever may be said only with many qualifications there is one thing that can be said for certain. It is that generally speaking the Senate's investigations have unquestionably hurt more than helped its reputation, entirely apart from all questions of the usefulness or lack of usefulness of the inquiries that it has made. The essential dignity of the Institution during these episodes has been injured beyond all reasonable argument, though it does not necessarily follow, therefore, that it should forever give up the investigative process. But no other activity, with the possible exception of the filibuster, has tended more often, justifiably or not, to bring the place into disrepute.

It may be that this is so because the mere act of inquiry, outside the framework of proposed legislation, is in some senses alien to the Senate: It was not set up to function as a grand jury, or even as a trial jury except in case of impeachments. And from the outstanding authorities on the subject a very good case could be made that the Senate was not granted anything approaching the limitless investigatory power that through the years it has asserted.

The Constitution itself, of course, said nothing specifically of *any* Senate right of investigation. Though it seems to have been universally conceded that some such privilege was inherent in a limited way since this body had the stated right to judge the qualifications of its own members, the first decade of the Institution's life had not passed before it proclaimed, the House of Representatives concurring, an explicit right going far beyond all this.

An act of 1798 empowered the Senate and the House through their committees to take testimony on oath and provided the usual "pains, penalties and disabilities" of perjury for those giving false testimony. Nothing was said here about the witness who refused to appear, or refused to talk when he had appeared. It was not until 1857 that provision was made legally for holding such witnesses in contempt.

In all the years since—years often of violent contentions between the Senate and the Executive Branch or the Senate and individual men—the Supreme Court has never affirmed, without qualification, the propriety of the Senate's investigative processes as related to its general right to supervise an administration. Nevertheless, no Senate committee has ever been prevented outright by any court from taking whatever action it had in mind against any individual, though committees have been checked after the deed was done.

Indeed, a century and a half of learned arguments and

court decisions have shown the bench far less than inclined to intervene against the Senate which, because of its nature as the superior forum, has far outshown the House in the celebrity and heat of its inquiries.

The Senate for itself in all that time has never clearly pushed to the ultimate implications its traditional claim that it has a right to demand any testimony of any sort or papers of any sort from the Executive Department. The Executive Department over and over has refused; the Senate over and over has fumed in retort—but then left the matter there.

Hard-pressed Presidents for many years have leaned most of all on what Andy Jackson, himself an old but irregular Senate man, wrote to a House rather than a Senate committee in 1837 when it called upon him to provide a great clutch of data on "all officers or agents or deputies" he had appointed in a given period—or, more bluntly, for information as to what he had been doing about political patronage.

". . . In open violation of the Constitution and of that well established and wise axiom that all men are presumed to be innocent until proven guilty," Jackson wrote, "you request myself and the Heads of Departments to become our own accusers. . . .

"The Heads of Departments may answer such a request as they please, provided they do not withdraw their own time and that of the officers under their direction from the public business to the injury thereof. . . . For myself, I repel all such attempts as an invasion of the principles of justice, as well as of the Constitution, and I shall esteem it my sacred duty to the people of the United States to resist them as I would the establishment of a Spanish Inquisition."

This bellicose, if not succinct, mouthful carried the day and historically has had perhaps more influence on the body to which it was not openly directed, the Senate, than the body to which it was sent, the House. A Senate-House committee investigating the Pearl Harbor disaster, under total domination from the Senate wing of the panel, had occasion grimly to recall this precedent when President Harry S. Truman publicly instructed the Executive Department to decide what papers were to be made available as "material to the investigation."

If Presidents have fared well in defying Senate committees, however, other men have not. Recalcitrant men were sent to jail in the Teapot Dome investigation and many have been morally destroyed since that time for refusing information to Senate investigating committees.

What has been actually established as to the extent of their power runs more nearly toward the limitless than the limited. The line of court decisions is to these practical effects: That Senate (or Congressional) investigations proceed from the general legislative authority. That power to compel disclosures is implied in this Constitutional grant of legislative authority. That the courts must "assume" when the Senate orders an investigation that it has a legislative purpose in doing so. That an investigation may be as broad as this implied legislative purpose seems to require. That the Senate may enforce its own processes. That the investigation is not limited to evidence that would have value in a court. That witnesses may be prosecuted for mistakes of law in refusing to answer. That members of a Senate investigation are immune to prosecution for falsely arresting a witness. That a witness is not privileged to refuse to produce a paper simply because it would tend to degrade him. That the life of a Senate investigation extends in fact as long as the Senate alone may decide.

All this complex of power explains the fact that investigations by the Senate so often proceed in an atmosphere far removed from that of a court. Not only is the Senate not bound by the same procedures; in many cases such procedures would be both unnecessary and destructive of the Senate objective. But there are, of course, instances—for example where a man's character and possibly his livelihood are at stake—where they would appear quite necessary but nevertheless do not exist.

For Senate investigations are of several distinctive types. The first and most common is simply that inquiry already mentioned which seeks the largely impersonal facts of a situation in advance of lawmaking—the most useful, the most bread-and-butter and the least criticized of all. Then there is the investigation into suspected misconduct in the Executive Department, as illustrated by the Teapot Dome and the Pearl Harbor inquiries. Finally, there is the investigation into the acts or associations of individuals, in or out of Government.

The Institution's investigative function thus has many and mixed purposes, supervisory or punitive, relatively objective in motive or wholly partisan and designed to promote or retard an administration, a policy or a concept. Again on occasion the purpose is primarily to ventilate a situation— to quiet a great public clamor or public fear. It therefore follows that flat and final judgments as to the value of the Senate investigation, viewed as an institutional function, are hard to come by. Ultimate truth is not here.

There is, for example, the undoubted fact that, rules or no rules, reform in procedure or no reform, the rights of a witness in a Senate investigation are really only about what the chairman says they are. (Operations in the House are more nearly governed by regulations; there is also the circumstance that there a powerful Speaker in the last analysis stands over all that is done.) No accused man has any fixed right of cross-examination, though his lawyer may, at the will of the committee, be allowed some pale imitation of cross-examination as practiced in a court. No accused man, or his counsel can control the timing or the presentation of his side of the case, and thus to any degree control its impact upon the channels of information. For an illustration, a Senate committee may pile up the damning aspects of the matter for hours or days, if it chooses, to extract its maximum effect, and then permit the accused to make an answer the usefulness of which or the striking nature of which has been almost wholly ruined by the passage of time.

Hearsay evidence is commonplace and allusive information is as often present, if not more often, than clear, positive information. The whole affair endures as long, or as briefly, as the committee itself may determine. The man under inquiry cannot move to adjourn; he cannot, really, move at all.

It is often argued, with great weight to many, that no Senate inquiry literally tries a man and that there is no reason to suppose that its processes will or should be the processes of a court. The contention undoubtedly makes much sense in regard to most types of Senate investigations —that is, those in which not mainly men but mainly issues or circumstances are under examination and trial. To one who has seen many investigations of the personal type, however, it is not convincing to say that the men in the dock in this sort of inquiry are not "on trial." They are in simple human truth very much on trial; worse yet, they run the inevitable hazards of a trial without any of its accompanying safeguards.

And all this, it should be emphasized, is the case not only with investigations conducted by men like Senator McCarthy from the right wing but by inquiries run from the liberal or left wing. It is not simply State Department officials and liberal professors who are put through these processes; it is also on occasion businessmen or men whose pasts, however criminal, have not left them unentitled to the protection of the Bill of Rights.

Senate investigations *can* be "witch hunts," all right, whether the witch be a pink intellectual or a florid ex-bootlegger with a picturesque underworld name caught in an equally blinding light from the television batteries. But this is only one side of the story. Senate investigations also can be of demonstrable value to the country as means to halt pillage of the Treasury, as in Teapot Dome, or to halt hysteria endangering Constitutional principles as was the case in the inquiry headed by Senator Russell of Georgia into President Truman's recall of General Douglas MacArthur from Far Eastern command.

Again, as when Senator Nye of North Dakota and his associates pursued the so-called "Merchants of Death" in the munitions industry, Senate investigations can mold the intellectual climate of much of a whole country into supposing that because the private production of munitions had been accompanied by corruption it would be better to have no munitions so produced.

This is the most formidable, the most subtle, and, for all its potential for informing or misleading masses of men, perhaps the most indispensable of all forms of Senate inquiry. It is here that there exists a propaganda forum of incomparable influence capable, like such other forums as education and the press and radio, either of immense evil or immense good.

This sort of inquiry usually starts with certain preconceptions in the mind of its chairman and in the minds of what is nearly always a controlling number of his committee associates. In Senator Nye's case the preconception was one of an isolationist pacificism based on the belief that war was necessarily bad, that profits were its ugly seeds and, presumably, that since weapons were needed to wage war, war would be banished once weapons were banished. This curious oversimplification, so similar to the oversimplification that led to prohibition on the theory that liquor was always and necessarily bad, had incalculable effects in restricting the free world's preparations as Hitler was rising in Germany.

Pursuing his notion that the way to prevent war was to "take the profits out of war," Senator Nye's committee produced findings and recommendations filling more than fourteen hundred pages, and a majority at length favored nationalization of most of the munitions industry. A companion effort was made to prepare a case that the United States entered the First World War primarily because of the pressures of the private munitions makers.

A committee staff memorandum put into the record by Nye in substance indicted the United States itself and spoke much less harshly of a German enemy who within less than five years was to reopen a career of banditry ending in the Second World War. The United States was accused

236

of "complete lack of neutrality" and the Allies of "selfish and materialistic aspirations." This country was found to have been supplying "materials of murder" to the Allies "in unlimited quantities." Germany for her part was using unrestricted submarine warfare because in this lay her "only chance of success" and in the end "America's complete lack of neutrality was responsible."

The right of a Senator to make a case in debate for or against a policy not only is beyond question as a Constitutional matter; it is also true that in failing to exercise this right the Senate would be failing in one of its highest duties. The difficulty arises, certainly in practice if not in Constitutional theory, out of this fact: There is a vast difference between the degree of public acceptance of what is on the one hand frankly only a Senatorial *argument* and what on the other hand is presented as factual matter obtained on the witness stand with all the solemnity of information adduced under oath.

The situation is comparable to one in which the editorial views of some parts of the press are deliberately mixed and mingled with the reported facts in such a way as to offer these views not as mere opinion but as unchallenged verities.

And though recent experience has perhaps fostered the public notion that it is only bitter right-wing Senators who have a means for distorting issues and punishing men by the technique of investigation, there is no historical basis for supposing that the offenders come solely from that side.

237

The fact is that the Nye munitions investigation, for an example, was a *left-wing* manifestation as were other celebrated inquiries of the thirties in which personages as eminent as Supreme Court Justice Hugo Black participated as Senators.

The Pearl Harbor investigation of 1945, on the other hand, was instigated from the Senate right wing. Where Nye's activity had the effect, not intended, of helping to enfeeble the Western world before Hitler, the Pearl Harbor inquiry had the effect, not intended, of weakening and dividing the country in the twilight of the Second World War.

Where the slogan "Merchants of Death" played into the hands of the aggressors in Imperial Germany and to some extent served as justification for them, much of the effort in the Pearl Harbor investigation was to apologize for the Japanese, who after all did attack our Pacific bases before we fired a shot at them.

Over and over it may be seen, therefore, that Senate investigations of this kind not only proceed with little regard to true objectivity. Over and over it also may be seen that, for all the trappings of pseudo-justice with which they are surrounded, they produce in fact even more intemperate partisan strictures than does the unlimited and frankly uninhibited debate of the Institution itself.

To recognize this, however, is like recognizing the undoubtedly bad features of the filibuster. It is not to say that on balance this sort of investigation should be outlawed by the conscience of the country. It is fundamentally a defensible activity, just as is the filibuster.

For it is a fact that there have been periods in the country's life, and no doubt will be others, when an Executive Department and a public point of view have been or will be powerful enough to hide what truly should be disclosed or to forward policies that truly ought to be checked. When such times do arise there is literally no other instrumentality of Government to cope adequately with them. When, for illustration, one reads the compelling evidence of the administration of justice in the Harding Administration it is quite clear that the relief and vindication of the public interest could hardly have come from the Department of Justice or from anywhere else in that Administration.

The Supreme Court and the House of Representatives might have discerned a certain stench. The Court, however, is hardly in position to conduct inquiries and prosecutions; the House will rarely be found strong enough in essential prestige to do so against an entrenched administration. And, even granted the prestige, its personnel lacks that shelter from quick retaliation, whether instigated by the administration or the public, that characterizes the Institution.

It was for this latter reason of relative invulnerability that the Senate—both its parties—was able to perform with almost universally acclaimed utility and honor in the case of the Douglas MacArthur incident.

XVIII

SENATE INVESTIGATIONS, GOOD

WHEN in the spring of 1951 President Truman broke General of the Army Douglas MacArthur as our Supreme Commander in the Far East there suddenly opened perhaps the gravest and most emotional Constitutional crisis that the United States had known since the Great Depression. This is of course strong language. It rests not on the authority of this writer but on his conversations at the time with some of the most responsible and ordinarily imperturbable men in the Government of the United States in both the Legislative and Executive Branches.

The situation, though supremely different in its causes, was in effect and in atmosphere not dissimilar to the abdication crisis in Britain when Edward VIII left the throne, as he said, for the woman he loved. The issue there was the unwritten supremacy of Parliament over the monarch, resting on at least three hundred years of tradition. The issue here was the supremacy, written and unwritten, that a century and a half had given to the civil Government over the military. Involved, here as there, was the extraordinary appeal to ordinary people of a powerful personality—General MacArthur's here and Edward's there—and at a sad, nostalgic, perilous and wistful moment in history.

The United States was deep in the Korean War, and now, it seemed, we were about to lose to the intruding Chinese Communists the victory that with our associates we had largely won over the North Korean Communist aggressors. Not in the memory of the citizens had so bitterly strange a war been fought in the first place. This first example of collective fighting for collective security under the United

242

Nations had to be headed by a nation wholly without experience in the concept of limited warfare, torn by savage partisan dissension and led by a President, Mr. Truman, whose moral authority of headship had been and was under violent and largely effective attack. Not all the gallantry of this memorably lofty and selfless intervention against aggression was enough for the time to shed any glow about the Presidency.

To the contrary, General MacArthur returned to the United States in April, 1951, as the dashing symbol of all that much of the country had loved in warfare and of all that much of the country now felt lost—the color, the power, the decisiveness, the attainable victory which it felt had been "thrown away" by national kowtowing to foreign nations and to a "foreign" instrumentality, the United Nations.

The image of the peaked cap and the brooding eyes of the handsome general swept the United States, for a time, as no image had swept it in the lifetime of those in middle age. In New York 2,850 tons of torn paper fell in his honor, the heaviest ticker-tape shower on record and one dwarfing the 1,750 tons of genial litter that in 1927 had been loosed in honor of Charles A. Lindbergh.

The great difference was that Lindbergh had been greeted as a young man who had flown the Atlantic alone; the general was greeted as a senior officer in full uniform contemptuously defying a President of the United States and a Constitutional

243

Commander in Chief and undertaking to force alteration in the highest decisions of the civil Government of the United States.

When MacArthur spoke before a joint session of Congress, ending with his famous observation about the old soldiers who just fade away, the scene was one that was quite indescribable without the reckless use of superlatives. If one may be pardoned such personal references as are necessary to make the point, the atmosphere was the most curiously emotional I had ever seen in service as a correspondent including covering such matters as D-day in Normandy, the liberation of Paris, and the death of Franklin Roosevelt.

Sophisticated members of the assembled group of Senators and Representatives, including some of those opposed to MacArthur in principle and in policy, were observed openly to weep on the floor of the House. Women employees in the Capitol, not excluding those working for the party whose President had recalled General MacArthur, were wholly undone in freshets of tears. One of the most balanced and soundest public men I have ever known, a distinguished Senator of great personal and political reserve, said to me as we walked back to the Senate chamber from the House: "This is new to my experience; I have never feared more for the institutions of the country. I honestly felt back there that if the [general's] speech had gone on much longer there might have been a march on the White House."

If there was exaggeration in this for the purposes of emphasis it was not discernible.

It was in this general scene that the Senate set out in May of 1951 to make an investigation later so universally acclaimed as to offer a great argument for the continuance, however abused at times, of its general powers of inquest. Appointed to do the job was what amounted to a panel of the elite of the Institution, the combined memberships of the Senate Foreign Relations and Armed Services Committees under the chairmanship of Senator Russell of Georgia. There was at the onset a good deal of the usual purely partisan maneuvering. Efforts were made by the Republicans, for example, to throw the joint committee's hearings open to the public, with what undoubtedly was at least a secondary purpose of embarrassing the Truman Administration. The Democrats for their part successfully resisted open hearings, under the leadership of Senator Russell. Here, too, there was some partisan motive, if a quite reserved one, to shield the Administration. On the whole, however, it was the view of detached observers that primarily Russell simply was concerned with avoiding disclosures that would injure the national rather than the White House interest. The Republicans themselves came in the end to that view; they all ultimately joined in saluting Senator Russell for an able, a disinterested and a fair inquiry. While politics in the ordinary sense was clearly involved from time to time, the net effect was of a patriotic, informed and on the whole an effective group of Senators.

245

Russell at the outset was adamant against admitting television or even the press. Criticism at first was heavy, and especially from working members of the press, but the method hit upon by the committee was too fair, too informative and too orderly to permit this criticism to survive. It was arranged to hand out from the hearing room in the Senate Office Building a transcript of the whole proceedings, processed a page at a time and shorn only of military information that might have had a clear and present utility to potential or actual enemies.

The censorship was in the charge of a high-ranking and non-political naval officer whose instructions were to make his decisions with the utmost liberality, withholding only that which demonstrably could not be published in the highest of national interest. The whole of the proceeding was quiet, unruffled, orderly and, strangely at variance with the investigative habits of the Institution, conducted with a decorum that would have pleased the Supreme Court itself.

Those correspondents who had come prepared to scoff at the arrangement remained to praise it. It was, in all truth, a demonstration of what the Senate at its best was capable of doing.

The transcript, of course, as it came in one damp sheet at a time from the closed committee room, was not innocent of partisanship on both sides as it was not innocent of bitter statements and charges. To those who watched outside from day to day, however, full of their memories of other Senate investigations, it was soon clear that what was going on inside was genuinely an inquiry, not simply into the recall of one general but into the whole state of health of American foreign and military policy. The Republicans as a group, headed by Bridges of New Hampshire, did not spare Mr. Truman in their questions and their findings. Nevertheless, they all joined the Democrats in recognizing that beneath all the harsh issues as to whether General MacArthur's military recommendations were right or wrong—indeed beneath all questions as to whether we would win or lose the Korean War—stood a truly fundamental issue.

This issue was whether the Senate for the first time in history would give any comfort, however small, to a theory that any high policy, however wrong, could in the end be settled by military rather than civilian officials.

The Democrats on their side did not truly attempt to "protect" the Truman Administration, which was in fact in disfavor with most of them. On the other hand they did not attempt to prosecute General MacArthur. What they attempted and accomplished—what all on the joint committee attempted and accomplished—was the lancing of a boil that could have spread a grave infection over the whole national political body.

While the Republicans found much in Mr. Truman's policy and conduct to denounce, the extraordinary achievement of this inquiry was to adopt *unanimously* a message "To the

247

American People," drafted by Senator Russell, that almost overnight calmed the atmosphere.

"It has been asserted," said this great paper of state, "that the cleavages made evident by these hearings have caused confusion at home, dismayed and frightened the free peoples we hold as friends and lent encouragement to those who would destroy us.

"We believe that our democracy has the vitality to withstand any strains that reflect the tensions of an uneasy world. We are convinced that an open discussion of such differences in no wise alters the fact that our great objective is still to live within the family of nations as a free people.

"The Nation will take the record of the hearings. We will study it. We will draw conclusions. We may differ on the proper policy to be applied in the Far East. We may separate on questions of strategy. We may divide on personalities.

"But we will be united in our devotion to liberty and justice, be single-minded in our will to preserve our institutions. We hope they may be preserved in peace, but preserve them we shall. We will be together in the defense of our way of life against any alien aggressor.

"These hearings have increased our faith in our strength and in our ability. Mistakes may add to the measure of our sacrifices or change the form of the ordeal we may be called upon to endure, but come what may America has the means and the will to enable us to survive. Strengthened

248

by this conviction, let us reject all counsels of defeatism and despair."

Appended was a message "To the Free Nations" reassuring them that what had been going on in the United States was an indication not of weakness but of strength. Finally, "the Communist World" was then advised:

"If those who threaten us take only a tyrant's lesson from differences among free men and mistake the temper of our people they can plunge the world into war. But it would be a war they could never win and which would bring them to ultimate destruction.

"The issues which might divide our people are far transcended by the things which unite them. If threatened danger becomes war [meaning world war], the aggressor would find at one stroke arrayed against him the united energies, the united resources, and the united devotion of all the American people."

This manifesto was accompanied by a unanimous decision by the joint committee that whatever else lay in doubt there could be no doubt of one thing: The Senate wholly rejected any possible question of the President's *right* to act as he acted in bringing General MacArthur home.

What had been done here by the joint committee was not gladly done. To participate in that inquiry at that time was not a welcome assignment and Russell and his associates in this case sought not headlines but the performance of duty. Together they dissolved a national emotionalism the

249

exact like of which had not heretofore been seen.

They offered no conclusions in the ordinary sense, and the manifesto on which they all agreed *could* be held to be highly generalized in tone. All this, however, was quite conscious and purposeful. They went, both instinctively and deliberately, to the *one* overpowering issue in the affair. In the process, parenthetically, they protected not only the American tradition of the pre-eminent civil authority; they halted what was then an almost runaway movement toward rejection of the United Nations.

This latter achievement to some of the members was not conscious; some on the joint committee did not then or later genuinely support the United Nations. For all that, it was still a historic achievement, the finest service alike of Russell and all who served with him.

And the most important point of all is that no other instrumentality could have done all this, however high and determined its intentions. The Administration, suspect among all who felt that General MacArthur had been mistreated, found itself simply to be shouting down a wind tunnel in attempting to place the controversy upon a Constitutional basis. The ordinary Democratic party organizations were inclined to an all-out, indiscriminate defense of the President and an indiscriminate attack upon MacArthur that clearly would have only inflamed national feeling on both sides. The ordinary Republican party organizations were inclined to an all-out indiscriminate defense of General MacArthur, not bothering in the process to consider the precedent they were about to raise, and an indiscriminate attack upon President Truman.

It is always a tricky thing confidently to assert that any action at a given time in history had directly and indisputably a clear and immediate effect, but the effects here noted were visible to all who happened to be in position to observe the aftermath with full knowledge of what had gone before. Coincidently or not, a part of the aftermath was the almost incredible collapse at the Republican National Convention in 1952 of the boom for MacArthur for the Presidential nomination. On every side it had been expected that he would be a formidable candidate, capable at any time of setting off an irresistible MacArthur movement. Coincidently or not, the only group confident in advance that this movement would never come were members of the Senate.

Without rejecting outright a single MacArthur military policy, without defending at a single point a single Truman policy, without accusing the General of anything whatever, the Senate's investigation had largely ended his influence on policy-making. It had set in motion, by the nature of the inquiry, an intellectual counterforce to the emotional adulation that for a time had run so strongly through the country.

There was, so far as I know, no direct purpose anywhere to nullify General MacArthur as a political force. Nevertheless, the flame that burned so hotly for him was the quicker going out because of the investigation.

Re-examining the mechanics of that investigation, its essential characteristics were these: no kleig lights, no television, no spectacular examinations and cross-examinations, very little name calling except on a high plane, no hippodrome, no addressing a public that could not be there to hear. Since all that was absent there is commonly present, does it then follow that Senate investigations are good or bad in exact ratio to their decorum and good taste and sense of responsibility? This, too, is not necessarily so.

XIX

SENATE INVESTIGATIONS,

BAD

THE FIFTH AMENDMENT is widely, and to a degree correctly, thought to have been much abused in recent years by witnesses before Senate committees. What is not nearly so widely understood is the frequent abuse of that Amendment by Senate committees themselves. If one may venture an inexpert opinion, arrived at after long and intimate observation and not lightly entertained, it is this: No greater and more persistent extra-Constitutional usurpations of power have been seen in this country than the recurring usurpations under the Fifth Amendment by investigating committees operating on the authority and responsibility of the Institution.

All are familiar with one aspect of the Amendment, that which permits men to refuse to testify against themselves. But this privilege is neither the whole nor even the main part of the great proviso, which proclaims at the outset: "No person shall be held to answer for a capital, or otherwise infamous, crime *unless on a presentment or indictment of a Grand Jury.*"

If there is one precise kind of Senate investigation that can be said to be clearly and demonstrably bad it is that fairly frequent sort of inquiry that is punitive and in the spirit of prosecution. These tend to operate, whatever the motive, as parodies of grand jury proceedings, a fact in no way altered by the real or presumed evil nature of their victims. Again and again in history, these investigations which seem to be largely accepted by the legal profession as more or less sanctioned by time and practice, have gone where not even the most ruthless and ambitious district attorney would dare to go.

254

They have assaulted the privacy not merely of suspected subversives but of private business. They have made wholesale seizures of private papers that have looked remarkably like partisan or merely vindictive fishing expeditions. They have, on commercially sponsored television broadcasts, as was the case in 1951 of Senator Kefauver's "crime investigation," held up men to public scorn and contempt for having had *past* brushes with the law. They have intervened (one might readily say "interfered") in the *local* administration of justice over *local* crime. They have even sought to haul up governors of Constitutionally sovereign States to make answers to questions from Senatorial inquisitors whose right to ask them in the first place has to a layman seemed open to the greatest doubt. They have on occasion complicated the work of the lawful Federal investigative authorities and of the country's lawful intelligence agencies. They have given broad hints to the lawful prosecuting agencies and even to the courts themselves as to what they ought to do in certain cases.

While it cannot be denied that sometimes "results" of one sort or another have followed, equally it cannot be denied that most of the time there have been no results at all except for the aggrandizement of personal political careers. And even where "results" have been obtained, the price that has been paid has seemed open to legitimate question.

If there is indeed something unpleasant in the unmanly

spectacle of suspected Communists or ex-Communists or suspected boodlers hiding behind the Fifth Amendment, what is to be said for the distortion of that other part of the Fifth Amendment so often permitted in the place that most of the time so venerates the Constitution? From whom is the country entitled to expect more? From the furtive handful whose creed, if they possess one, is anti-Constitutional? Or from the Senate of the United States, the last, best home of due process short of the Supreme Court itself?

Many of legal lore and learning have written of this sort of investigation. This writer's observations, for the necessarily personal nature of which he must apologize, are those simply of a man wholly without legal training and qualified as a witness, if qualified at all, only because his profession has caused him to watch many of these inquiries at work from a seat more intimate than is available to the public.

Many investigations of this kind he has seen, investigations from the right and investigations from the left. It is his conclusion, for what it may be worth, that they are and must be *essentially unfair,* unfair not merely to left wingers and those who correctly or not call themselves intellectuals, but unfair to right wingers, free enterprisers—all who run afoul of this undue process.

And it is the conclusion, too, that the great majority of the Senate itself in its heart feels exactly the same way. The basic, the incurable trouble is that this is fatally the wrong forum for the business. The Senate simply has no *right* to indict men outside its rank or at most outside the Government. It has *every* right to indict issues, policies, systems, Executive Departments. It has the undoubted right and duty to act Constitutionally against those who may fail in their Constitutional duty to do that which the Institution itself should not do—to bring to account, for illustration, any departmental head who in truth permits subversion or corruption among his personnel. But the Senate's whole *raison d'être*, in so far as it is indirectly an agency of actual justice, is far removed from the prosecuting function. Its power to try impeachments is the power to weigh and dispense justice, not to inveigh for justice.

And because it has this unique power of final judgment— because it may at any time be called upon to sit as a high court of impeachment, it is possible to make out a case that even in its dealings with men within the Government, not to mention those outside, it owes a great reticence in conduct.

At all events, there is a deep and inevitable inherent disorder whenever and wherever the Senate sets out to punish or prosecute, in or out of Government.

This fact has been so fully and so endlessly illustrated by the so-called "Communist probes," conducted in the fifties by Senators McCarthy and McCarran and others, as surely to require no detailed illustration here. For many months in each of several years the very corridors of the

257

Senate Office Building—the site of the echoing marble Caucus Room where so many of these inquisitions were conducted—stank with the odor of fear and the odor of monstrous silliness.

The presumed and alleged objective was to seek out and destroy what was supposed to be a vast Communist "apparatus" that was gnawing at the Republic's vitals. The obvious and practical effect, however, was a long pursuit of individual men—and a sorry lot they were, on the whole—across this panorama of a bitter and foolish time in our history. There was a rarely changing cast of characters: There were the professional informers, nearly all of them recanted ex-Communists, in spirit howling of their quite doubtful virtue like field hands exulting in the salvation found at a Holy Roller meeting in the canebrakes. There were the inevitable props, the tired, metallic voices of the microphones, the beating kleig lights, the whole jargon of a shabby trade.

And then there were the men and women being pursued. What could one say of them, in retrospect? Some were by all appearances people of value and distinction to American life and in their cases the doubly tragic implications of these proceedings were all too clear. But some of them, perhaps most of them, were far from prepossessing, if viewed only as people and not also as people in an ugly kind of trouble. Some also indisputably had been Communists, some had been in one pink association or another, and some seemed to be simply of that hapless type who is invariably

258

the one to be run down by the traffic in witlessly crossing the street against the lights. The wry onlooker could, incidentally, take some comfort: If some of *these* were typical of the enemies of the Republic we had little to fear. They were, of course, not at all typical of the real enemy; they were for the most part just that sort of dismal crackpot or deluded neurotic that men more trained in hunting headlines than in hunting subversion would infallibly pick out.

But to say that it was difficult to find sympathy with them in the purely personal sense is not to say that one could withhold his concern at the assaults that occurred upon their indestructible (one hopes) American rights.

As for the Senate interrogators, never were so many vast charges made against so many with such piddling results; never did anticipation so outrun realization. The archetype among the victims of the era, for an example, was Professor Owen Lattimore. Mr. Lattimore not only turned out to be anything but that "top Soviet agent" whom he had been in Senator McCarthy's enfevered declarations; the courts stepped in to nullify a hysterical prosecution for perjury against the professor that the McCarran Committee had insisted upon in a usurpation of the proper functions of the Federal prosecuting arm.

It has, however, been a melancholy truth that national leaders and powerful organs of opinion, while properly condemning unfairness in the McCarthys of the Senate, have been remarkably soft with procedures that *in principle* have been no less unfair, in what might be called the reformer's type of investigation.

Through 1951 the Kefauver "Crime Committee" roamed importantly about the land in what a publication generally approving of its activities, *Time* Magazine, called "his road-show." The whole of the proceeding had the inescapable tone of being first and foremost a national entertainment. Housewives at the kitchen sink, peering over the automatic dishwasher; men in offices and taverns and bars—all took what amounted to a national quasi-holiday over this prolonged and extraordinary spectacle. What at length emerged from it all was more an aura of general accusation than the disclosure of any specific "crime" over which such a body as the United States Senate could have had any conceivable jurisdiction.

By way of example, *Time* Magazine, raptly describing Senator Kefauver's exploits in "trudging through California, doggedly intent on the trail of Big Crime," had this in part to say: "Before a massed bank of newspaper reporters and the peering snouts of television cameras, Kefauver has spent the afternoon listening, *as a motley crew of mobsters* admitted what they could not deny, chanted insolently when cornered: 'I don't remember.'

"Debonair Al Smiley, ex-partner of Mobster 'Buggsy' Siegel, inspected Kefauver contemptuously. He refused to say why, after Siegel's untimely death, a Houston man had asked him to come down to Texas, and why Smiley had shuttled back and forth between Houston and the Beverly Club, the gambling casino near New Orleans controlled by New York's Frank Costello. Smiley's reward for these questionable services was 'a small piece of property.' What kind of property? 'Well, it may have had a few oil wells on it,' said Al, and departed with a curled lip."

This was rich fare, especially that curled lip, but like so many of the achievements of the "Crime Committee" it was a little difficult to discover *precisely* what had been accomplished and *precisely* wherein lay the Senate's responsibility or mandate. The old unterrified, Senator Connally of Texas, had no trouble in giving his personal summary of what the committee was doing. "Off chasing crapshooters," he growled, in public.

In general, however, the Senate, embarrassed to its depth as it was, went along—as to an almost incredible length it will always go along with any one of its investigating instrumentalities.

In this brief, empurpled phase of our national life many of those who might have been adverse critics kept their silence; to criticize the "Crime Investigation" might have made one out to be pro-criminal just as to criticize "Communist investigations" was to run the risk of being put down as pro-Communist.

The Kefauver Committee, which had personnel innately decent but also innately melodramatic, produced for the country a whole rogues' gallery of men without proper Anglo-Saxon names, men with criminal records and other men simply characterized in much of the press as "gangsters" without supporting data. It produced, too, a re-emergence of that spirit of avid puritanism that still lies so close to the top of the national life.

The committee was interrogating—though the word is a bit euphemistic for a procedure that offered hand-twisting, grunting, inarticulate, captive, involuntary actors who no doubt had contributed little that was good to their society—men who were in the true sense friendless before the country. It was all too easy to condemn them, in this the first trial by television in the history of the United States, for they were for the most part incontestably "bad" men. Few, however, if any, in responsible place rose to remark that the Bill of Rights was designed for bad as well as good men, even more perhaps for the bad than the good. The victims in the State Department and the universities of another aspect of this type of punitive investigation were much and properly agonized over by the right-thinkers; few could spare anxiety for the wretched victims of the Crime Investigation.

For in the true and Constitutional sense they, too, were victims, victims of a usurpation of a power belonging only to grand juries under the Fifth Amendment. If they had broken the law they were accountable to these juries, but to these alone until indictments were brought. None was properly accountable to a national revival meeting of indecent self-righteousness bathed in incandescent light on a stage having sanction neither in the Constitution nor in the tradition of a people.

Even the courts—and I have undertaken to show how very reluctantly they will intervene against the inquiries of the Institution—could not stand this much this time. The Kefauver Committee hurled contempt citations right and left, and the Senate for the most part shamefacedly confirmed them. But the courts took a different view.

The authoritative research organ *Congressional Quarterly Almanac* dryly observes: "The number of contempt-of-Congress citations voted in 1952 (eight) was considerably smaller than that approved in 1951, when the Senate Crime Investigating Committee cited forty-five persons for contempt.

"The Courts meanwhile were turning down many of the cases brought against persons cited. . . . About twenty men cited by the Senate Crime Committee in 1951 were acquitted or had earlier convictions reversed in 1952 by the Courts, which generally upheld pleas of possible self-incrimination in refusing to answer questions."

From all this scene, this scene of the extra-Constitutional punishment by the Senate of individual persons over whom it has no fit mandate to sit in judgment, emerge three important and gloomy facts. The first is the failure of political liberalism to defend true liberal values in all their context—and not merely in those cases where the transgressed are themselves friends of liberalism and thus "acceptable," like the professors or the diplomatic career people. For the bad and the friendless—these, too, bleed from the wound of injustice.

The second is the failure, the grievous failure, of political conservatism, which has the greater responsibility because it has the greater attachment to order and tradition, to lift a single effective concert of voices at unfairness at any point, whoever the victim.

The third and worst of all is the shame of the Senate itself, as a guardian of the great Constitutional traditions, in condoning what it *knows* is not right.

These failures have not, of course, occurred only in our generation, but history does indicate that in this period they have become both more frequent and more aggravated. And in this process of accelerating irresponsibility and ultimate lawlessness in a single unhappy field lies, I believe as a basically sympathetic observer, one of the two great dangers to the continued ascendancy of the Institution in the higher public life of the Republic.

It is only this kind of irresponsibility, and one related kind of which mention shortly will be made, that can erode the moral base on which the Senate in the end must stand and which once crumbled could not in many lifetimes be rebuilt in strength and durability. For the Senate in a way is on a long probation, a tenable place only through a Constitutional understructure that for all its incomparable

264

stability is already under quite enough stress in the political evolution of the United States. This evolution, this movement of the present and the future, is wholly away from the central concept of the Senate. This Senate concept, as has been seen, heavily *qualifies* democracy. The irresistible movement for now and for the foreseeable tomorrow demands the vast and steady expansion of at least a kind of democracy—call it a true enlargement, as most now may do, or call it both an enlargement and an attenuation of democracy in which, perhaps, the whole is distantly jeopardized by the growing and tragic disharmony between ill-exercised responsibilities and over-exercised privileges and rights.

That this overpowering demand exists is recognized by many in the Senate and recognized, too, is the second of the twin dangers. This danger lies in the clear and frequent abuse of Senatorial immunity from action for libel or slander for what is said in committees or on the floor.

Article I of the Constitution, in saying of members of the Senate and House alike that "for any Speech or Debate . . . they shall not be questioned in any other place," was intended mainly to prevent harassment of legislators by the Executive authority as Parliament once protected itself from such harassments by a King. As is common knowledge, however, the area of immunity has become broadened to the point where without the slightest legal liability a Senator may destroy a reputation in an ill-considered, malicious or simply angry sentence.

265

It is difficult to believe that so vast and total a sanctuary was intended by the Founders, and it is increasingly obvious that the people are not willing to accept anything of the kind. And the issue as a practical matter never arises when the Institution is about its fundamental and true business, but it endlessly arises in the sort of investigation that has been under examination here. The oftener it arises the more difficult it will be to put off the question with the valid argument that Senate debate is and must be unlimited. Indeed it is, and indeed it must be. But again, the real authority of the Senate is at bottom a moral-Constitutional authority and this authority itself rests at last upon a great, single ideal, the ideal of fair play. The ethic of the people will not, one believes, forever countenance violation of that ideal from on high. It is well to recall that the ancient institution of kingship fell most of all because too many kings so ill equated responsibility with privilege.

In summary, then, to deal with the whole aspect of the Senate's function of investigation, the finding is this. Inquiry to supervise and even to attempt to force policy change upon the Executive is indispensable and ought not to be disturbed, though the Senate owes the country a ceaseless vigilance over its processes. Inquiry for the making of propaganda, even "bad" propaganda, is indispensable. Inquiry for the connected purposes of punishing individuals and promoting Senatorial publicity is more bad than good, wherever the almost inevitable Constitutional usurpations occur. It is more bad

266

1 CITY PACKING SLIP 2.20

PP .68
TAG
2.10
2.30

BOOKS

for

FROM:

HARPER & BROTHERS

307 ASH STREET, SCRANTON 9, PENNA.

S028539

than good even though it may fall out that without such investigations some subversives may go uncaught and some spoilers may go undetected. For detection is not the function of the Institution and there is in the great governmental House of the Republic a proper place for the exercise of each of the complex of powers. Better a House strongly standing at its foundation, even with some disorder in the eaves, than a most orderly House fatally wrenched about at its very base.

INDEX

268

269

271

National Association of Manufacturers, 144
natural gas lobbies, 145
nature and composition of the Senate, 22, 28
necessities, political, 76
Negroes, 3-4, 62, 63
  desegregation decision, 192
  equality, postponement of legislation, 64
Neuberger, Senator Richard, 188
New Deal, 148, 155, 174, 175, 176, 219
New Freedom, 219
newcomers, 82-83, 114, 115
newspapers, correspondents, 167-168
  influence on the Executive and on the Senate, 167
night sessions, 85
Norris, Senator George W., 17, 60, 64
North Atlantic Treaty Organization, 52
Nye, Senator Gerald P., 235, 236, 238

officials and pages, 147
oleomargarine, taxes on, 138
O'Mahoney, Senator Joseph C., 22
"operating," 209
origin, 22, 27-40
orthodoxy, party, 93
Outer and Inner Club, 86-87, 90

pacifism, 236
pages and officials, 147
parliamentarianism, 29, 74, 89
parties, social, diplomats', 170
  splinter, 185, 188
  two-party system and committee system, 185
partisanship, 24
party, accommodation, 106
  allegiance to, 98-106
  and Senate, 163-164
  independence from, 101
  pressure, 149-151
  Senate above party, 96
Pastore, Senator John O., 93
patriotic organizations, lobbies, 145
pay of Senators, 34
Payne, Senator Frederick G., 90-91
Pearl Harbor, 231, 233, 238
  investigating committee, Senate-House, 231

Penrose, Senator Boies, 144
"people," distrust of, 31
People's Party, 185
Pepper, Senator Claude, 4-5
  rebuke by Byrd, 79
perquisite, and abuse of, 41-53, 114-115
personalities, 199-211
personality. See individuality
physicians' lobby, 143
Pierce, President Franklin, 218
Pinckney, Senator Charles C., 69, 125
Poland, 162
policy committees, 210
Polk, Senator Truster, 124
popular elections (Seventeenth Amendment), 33
Populists, 185
Powell, Senator Lazarus W., 124
power, abuse of, 17-18
  Federal, Senate, and the individual, 109
  kernel of, 179-197
  not based on bigness, 15-16
  of veto, by minority, 62
powers, proposed, 34-35, 37
precedent, power of, 85
presence, sense of, 70, 72
President, the
  addresses to joint sessions, 43, 46
  "agent" of the Senate, 35
  alienation from, 158-159
  ambition, Senatorial, 85-86
  and the Constitution, 10-11
  and the Senate, 3, 10-12, 44, 86, 97-101, 162, 200, 213-225, 230
  and the Supreme Court, 224-225
  appointments and removals, proposed Senate veto power, 46-49
  attitude on rules of progress, 57
  differences with, 9-10
  dinners at the White House, 170
  election by bigness, 15
  Electoral College, 15
  few Presidents from the Senate, 213-225
  good, 219
  impeachment actions, 3
  opposition to, 156
  perquisites, 45-46

President—Cont.
  pressure by, 139
  receptions, 45-46
  South, the, and nominations, 215-216
  strong, 11-12
  transiency, 12
  treaty making, 35-36
  visits to the Senate, 1, 50
President of the Senate, pro tem, 147
Presidential campaign of 1956, 104
pressure, by Senators on constituents, 153-164
  on Senators, 135-151
priests, influence of, 143
primacy of the Senate, 38
principles, 115
privilege, 122, 123
privileges, of Senators, 122, 123
  of seniors, 83
probation, 264-265
progress, 55-56
Prohibition Amendment (Eighteenth), 28, 236
propaganda, 19, 143, 157, 160, 235-236, 266
propriety, 86
public not always right, 19-20
public utilities, lobbying, 146
Public Works, Committee on, 188
punishment and crime, 121-133
puritanism, 262
pursuit and perquisite, 41-53

qualifications, 2, 117-120, 159, 219
quarrelsomeness, x
quorums, 42

railroad workers' strike, 5
Rayburn, Speaker Sam, 33, 216
reaction, 116
Reciprocal Trade Program, 137
Reconstruction, 22, 62, 68
"Red hunters," 108
re-election. See election
reforms, 71
"regency, Senate," 223
removal, causes for, 124
Republican Committee on Committees, 182
Republican Conference, 182
Republican National Committee, 96
Republican party, contributions to, 146

274

42361